Also by Frederick Glaysher

The Parliament of Poets: An Epic Poem

The Bower of Nil: A Narrative Poem

Into the Ruins: Poems

The Grove of the Eumenides: Essays on Literature, Criticism, and Culture

Letters from the American Desert: Signposts of a Journey, A Vision

Crow Hunting: Songs of Innocence

Edited

Robert Hayden, *Collected Prose*; *Collected Poems*

The Myth of the Enlightenment

The Myth
of the
Enlightenment

Essays

Frederick Glaysher

Earthrise Press

I thank the editor of *Rupkatha Journal* (Vol. 3, No. 4. Spring 2012), Kolkata, India, for publishing my essay on Tagore. The two pieces on Robert Hayden were delivered at the University of Michigan and Wayne State University for events marking his centenary. The review on Fang Lizhi was read at the Midwest Conference on Asian Affairs. Most of the other essays and reviews have appeared on my blog, The Globe, or elsewhere, such as the interview on *Poets' Quarterly* with Arthur McMaster, to whom I also express my gratitude.

www.fglaysher.com

Glaysher, Frederick, 1954-
   The Myth of the Enlightenment: Essays / Frederick Glaysher. — 1st ed.
        p. cm.
Library of Congress Control Number: 2014944288
        ISBN: 978-0-9826778-3-4 (hardcover)
        I. Title.

PS3557.L37 M98 2014   814/.54   894222171

Earthrise Press®
P. O. Box 81842, Rochester, MI 48308-1842 USA
EarthrisePress.Net

For Dr. Hans-George Ruprecht

Contents

III Race in America

Preface

For over three-hundred years, civilization has been under the sway of the Myth of the Enlightenment. While the Enlightenment initiated a highly beneficial movement away from autocratic government and religion, a stifling reliance on past authorities, accompanied by an ever-increasing scientific and practical development, very early on stress and cracks began to be felt in the structure of the psyche and society. The twentieth century witnessed those cracks transmogrifying into crevasses of gaping and violent proportions, often circling the globe.

The last few decades have borne all the more testimony that the Myth of the Enlightenment has become part of the problem and no longer sufficiently comprises what is needed to resolve and heal what civilization is suffering from.

Speaking broadly, to reach the imagination of the entire culture, the cultural richness and plenitude of the humanities are essential and must include all of the religious and wisdom traditions. Story, myth, and drama reach the deepest into the psyche, as Carl Jung, Joseph Campbell, among others, understood, as they had learned from the greatest works of art and myth that were in fact at the core of their own studies.

Science cannot alone heal the divide that it, too, suffered as a result of the upheavals of the seventeenth century and modernity, though Quantum Physics suggests a transition of worldview. Neither can literature and the humanities alone heal the wound of civilization. It can only be done together, an act in itself that at last demonstrates the divide has been crossed, dramatizing it, as it were, for all to understand.

Ultimately, resolution can only come about, for the entire social sphere, through literature and culture, at the most sensitive levels, bearing a sense of history, of the past, as well as, again, a sense of the new scientific worldview implicit in Quantum Physics. Believing all that, I chose the epic form because of its universality, its presence in most major cultures, and its ability to carry the burden of epochal reassessment and transformation, through "wisdom and delight," which it repeatedly demonstrated in the past.

By dramatizing those antinomies, like life itself, beheld in a mirror, as it were, I believe we can imaginatively choose change, in consciousness, change consciousness, leading to, and helping to make more possible, adjustments in reality, which we all so dearly need around the world.

The planet has repeatedly told the 21st Century that it is most emphatically alive, Gaia become a Fury, beginning with the astounding earthquakes of Aceh, Indonesia and the Tohoku region of Japan, leading to devastating tsunamis, and multiple nuclear meltdowns in Fukushima that are still poisoning the atmosphere and oceans. Earlier, in 2001, the destruction of the Twin Towers of the World Trade Center by terrorists had opened the century with the demonstration that all had not become sweetness and light after the surprising and relatively peaceful demise of the Soviet Union, while the greed of unrestrained capitalism has become a cult and curse upon the face of the Earth.

Expanding on my literary criticism in *The Grove of the Eumenides (2007)*, these essays and reviews, including on race in America, have all been written during the 21st Century, grappling with and evincing the tumultuous changes in the psyche of the culture. They were all part of my evolving thinking while working on and writing my epic poem, *The Parliament of Poets*.

July 8, 2014

I The Myth of the Enlightenment

"Of True Religion" and John Milton

In 1673, a year before his death, John Milton published a pamphlet entitled *Of True Religion, Heresy, Schism, Toleration, and what the best means may be used against the Growth of Popery*. His great poems were all behind him, death before him. Oddly, this pamphlet is little known to the general reader of Milton. After looking through a number of textbook collections of Milton for university courses, published during the last several decades, I was surprised to discover none of them contained *Of True Religion*, yet it was the last piece the man ever wrote. All the more startling is that *Of True Religion* presents a portrait of John Milton significantly at variance with the Puritan caricature of him that is often promoted by scholars in the university. All too often Milton is torn out of his historical time and not seen to be in fact the liberal that he was, clearly headed toward the Glorious Revolution of 1688, which further limited the monarchy and prepared the way for the modern efflorescence of individual liberty and freedom. To distort Milton into a one-dimensional Puritan suppresses the complexity of his actual thinking and life.

Since I visited in the summer of 2009 Milton's home in Chalfont St. Giles, where he had lived fleeing the London plague of 1665, he was on my mind in the fall, and I was browsing online to see what I could turn up about him. I stumbled onto *Of True Religion* when I had downloaded a 19th Century edition of Milton's prose, published in 1826, from Google Books. There it was in the table of contents. I suppose it was still possible back then for "true religion" to exist. How curious. I looked in my 1977 college edition of Merritt Y. Hughes' *Complete Poems and Major Prose*, first published in 1957. Apparently, not major. In his opinion. After transferring it to my Sony Reader, to my surprise, I found Milton talking about toleration, leaving alone the "Lutherans, Calvinists, Anabaptists, Socinians" and Arminians, instead of persecuting them, harrying them out of the land, emphasizing what is held in common, versus sectarian. And how far should they be tolerated? "Doubtless equally, as being all Protestants." He further stressed they should be allowed to preach and argue in their assemblies, public writings and printing. From our perspective, one might say, of course, but Milton was progressive and on the advancing edge of his day. To fail to recognize that fact obscures who he was.

Milton's qualification is Protestantism. It's fair to say Milton does not have much warmth of feeling for "popery," or Catholicism in general, tending to vehement and even feverish denunciation. He's concerned, like many in his time, with the grasping for "usurped" ecclesiastical and political power. He calls to mind for his readers England's history under Catholicism when he writes that the pope "was wont to drain away the greatest part of the wealth of this then miserable land . . . to maintain the pride and luxury of his court and prelates." Milton was not the kind of man to take lightly the "Babylonish yoke" of popery, or anything else for that matter. My English genes cannot but thrill in agreement and admiration for his spirited defense of liberty. However, it's safe to say that while Milton was willing to extend freedom of conscience to fellow Protestants, which many of the time were not, he indubitably would have thought differently when it came to Buddhists, Muslims, Hindus, and people of other persuasions, lumping them all in there somewhere with popery—"idolatrous." The ruined abbeys all over England stand witness to both the extent of Catholic exploitation and the fierce backlash it inspired. Milton is tame by comparison. But no universality for him. Milton was convinced he had the exclusive truth in Protestantism.

Similarly, some today, trying to revive or return to Christianity, as a dominant social organization, celebrate Milton, thinking he is the way back to an idealized past. But the past is past because it is past. There's no going back in that direction. Why would one want to? Partly coming out of the

Enlightenment, the democratic pluralism of our time is much more dynamic and exciting, and, here's the important fact, true. True religion, in our time, must recognize the non-exclusivism of religious truth—that all peoples, religions, and traditions taught and held, still hold and teach, to the degree they're not atrophied or undermined by the nihilism of modernity, the same universal, spiritual insights, ideals, virtues, and truths. Far from exclusivism, far from the historicism and nihilism that attempts to discredit all religions and wisdom traditions, I aver, not that all religions are false, but that they're all true. I feel the rich heritage that we carry with us has become open to everyone around the globe, so that instead of only one exclusive tradition, if you will, we human beings have been becoming for a long time now increasingly heirs of all the past forms of transcendence. Far from their being swept aside, what is universal in them has become increasingly clarified so that it can be seen and appreciated as universal, an infinite Unity and Oneness, the global heritage of humanity.

With a nod to the long line of both Croatian Catholics and persecuted French Huguenots that I also come from, I would say the great religions all provide a vision and understanding of the purpose of life, what it means to be a human being, that is deeply profound, non-utopian, non-quixotic, when properly understood, of how and why one journeys through this world. We need to know as much about the Unknowable Essence as possible, from every angle, every insight into Divine Mystery, that we might come to understand Him or Her or It, just a little bit more. I'm not willing to settle for anything less than the fullness of Being, striving for It. To relinquish the thousands of years of human meditation on the Divine Being would be too great a loss. What then the point of life? The Exclusive Truth is beyond all attempts to understand Him. I also argue for retention of all the nay-sayers, atheists, agnostics, and nihilists. They have an important part of the truth to tell, while having no more the exclusive truth than anyone else. Relax, there's no reason to burn them at the stake or blow them up. Nor anyone.

While Milton urges Protestants, "who agree in the main," to show forth "forbearance and charity one towards the other," I would urge forbearance and charity for all, all the great religions and traditions, for this is what the logical, rational, reasonable development of modern democratic pluralism has already done, though we do not, I think, sufficiently recognize and celebrate it for the highly significant achievement that it is. Too often, global society continues, in a sense, to think and act in terms of exclusivism, whether religious or secular, while more often, in its lived experience, rightly recognizing and respecting the multifarious ways and paths through life. To make our achievement more conscious and acknowledged, indeed, more than mere toleration, celebrated, is one of the challenges and goals of the 21st Century, all times, and a path toward universal peace and understanding. Understandably, the countervailing fear is usually about organization. But in the modern world people have increasingly come to realize that true religion is merely an "attitude toward divinity," a frame of mind, a reverence for life, not an organization, best manifested as a distinctive quality of the individual.

Putting aside organizations and institutions, Milton writes, "True religion is the true worship and service of God, learnt and believed from the word of God only." Unfortunately drawing from Paul of Tarsus, Milton embraces some of Paul's more personal ideas and interpretations, and of the early Christian church, "to reject all other traditions," instead of universality. Similar to the harm Paul's teachings on misogyny have caused throughout the centuries, Paul's bifurcation of humanity, into the "elect" and the "wayward," has caused incalculable suffering and misery, all in the name of putative truth. All of the various forms in various traditions that have approached human nature in a similar manner have resulted invariably in analogous distortions and social dislocations, though Paul's many good acts and writings conducive to cultivating love and community are timeless. Milton is at his best when he's following what is universal in the Christian tradition.

Milton's other prose writings helped disenfranchise the church from the state. He and the time understood well the threat and result of fanatical exclusivity in power, or grasping for it, as we do living now, as a result of the fanatical exclusivism of Islamist terrorism, reminding us of how serious all these issues really are. Separation of church and state is one of the undeniably great achievements of the Enlightenment and civilization, even, I would say, the Will of God. From lived experience, life just goes better when matters of conscience and belief are balanced with different viewpoints, consultation, people of various religious outlooks, and no religious faith or belief, the full range of human thought and belief; the great pool of humanity, swirling around, trying to make sense of it all, no one shoving their exclusive truth down anyone else's throat, over the barrel of a gun, or with a bomb, their own form of organizational control, religious or secular. What could be more obvious about our actual experience of what works, what produces a peaceful, harmonious society, or, at least, as close as we can get to one in this world? Even for John Milton, the great fear was slipping back into popery or anything oppressive and tyrannical. At times, Milton was clearly not pleased with Oliver Cromwell, as attested and documented by Anna Beer in her biography of Milton. Not liberal by our standards today, but he was, by those of his own time, and headed in the direction of universality.

Tolstoy and the Last Station of Modernity

After seeing in early 2010 the movie "The Last Station," by the director Michael Hoffman, based on Leo Tolstoy's final year of life and his death at the train station of Astapovo in 1910, I found my thoughts often turning to him. I've had a long interest in Tolstoy and his work, having spent considerable time as a student reading large swaths of his journals and other more obscure books during the early 1970s and repeatedly going back to him during intervening years. While the acting of Helen Mirren and Christopher Plummer was superb, the latter of whom I admire having seen Plummer perform live a couple of times at the Stratford Shakespeare Festival in Canada, the movie left me with an uneasy feeling regarding the interpretation of Tolstoy. The film script was based on Jay Parini's novel, *The Last Station*, which may be part of the problem, in turn perhaps tracing back to the unsympathetic biographies by Henry Troyat and A. N. Wilson, both derisively presenting Tolstoy as a religious crank and fanatic. Neither biography understands the full weight of who Tolstoy was and what he actually believed and why. Touching on the problem, fearing other biographers would repeat the errors of Troyat, Tolstoy's daughter Alexandra wrote in 1968, in *The Real Tolstoy*, that "Troyat . . . shows no respect for Tolstoy's inner life. He speaks about it in vulgar, cynical expressions…. I fear that the errors in Troyat's book will be repeated in other works." Beyond the biographies, skewing also the movie, lies the pervasive nihilism and cynicism of modernity that have no respect or appreciation for any spiritual vision of life, including even a highly universal one, such as Tolstoy's, for he had embraced, by the last decade of his life, the universal principles and teachings, not only of Christianity, but of all the great religions. To see or set him in a more limited context is to fail to understand him within his own stated terms and the plenitude and scope of his work.

Born of aristocratic lineage, Tolstoy inherited his elite position in Russian society, along with the enormous estate of Yasnaya Polyana, south of Moscow. At thirty-four in 1862, he married Sophia Behrs, when she was eighteen years old. By all accounts they lived a happy domestic life together for many years. After his crisis of faith, discussed in *My Confessions* (1878), while he found the answers for his spiritual and intellectual struggles in his religious studies and books, they began to experience an increasingly strained relationship. Sophia's personality was much given, as she described herself, to the lightness of the social world she had been born into, growing up in Moscow in the circles of the Tsar's court. By her own recognition, Tolstoy had a much deeper inner life of the mind and sensibility. Their relationship was often strained for the rest of their lives. Torn between love and gratitude to her and a desire to bring his life and ideals in line with his beliefs, he and Sophia struggled on together. In a letter dated June 8, 1897, found concealed in his study after his death, published in Paris in *Figaro*, December 27, 1910, which Tolstoy apparently had never sent to Sophia, Tolstoy dreamed about leaving her and explained his motives better than he eventually did when he actually left her more than a decade later:

> For a long time, dear Sophie, I have been suffering from the discord between my life and my beliefs. I cannot force you to change your life or your habits. Neither have I hitherto been able to leave you, for I felt that by my departure I should deprive the children, still very young, of the little influence I might be able to exert over them, and also that I should cause you all a great deal of pain. But I cannot continue to live as I have lived, during these last sixteen years, now struggling against you and irritating you, now succumbing myself to the influences and the seductions to which I am accustomed and which surround me. I have resolved now to do what I have wished to do for a long time: to go away. . . . Just as the Hindoos, when they

arrive at the sixtieth year, go away into the forest; just as every aged and religious man, wishes to consecrate the last years of his life to God and not to jesting, punning, family tittletattle, and lawn-tennis, so do I with all my strength desire peace and solitude, and if not an absolute harmony at least not this crying discord between my whole life and my conscience. (*Tolstoy*, Romain Rolland, 181)

Tolstoy similarly once wrote to his sister, who was a nun in the Russian Orthodox Church, "How fine for the Buddhist when he grows old—he goes off to the desert." It was to his sister and the Shamardino monastery that Tolstoy first fled in 1910, though he quickly gave up on the notion of staying there and headed south towards his summer home in the Crimea. What is often lost sight of in our disbelieving age is that religious retreat in advanced years was an ideal that Tolstoy respected and wished to honor in fact and deed. Sophia, it should be noted, was diagnosed by more than one doctor as mentally ill, a fact recognized by his son Sergei in a letter to his father, after his flight in 1910, acknowledging that it would have been better had they separated many years earlier. The movie fails to do justice to this complexity, presenting Sophia as far too much the victimized realist of an impractical zealot of a husband. What has come to be a common interpretation of Tolstoy is completely false. That Tolstoy could continue to study and write under such conditions is a testament to the strength and integrity of his character and soul.

Like many writers, Tolstoy anguished, for years, over his inability to bring his life into balance with his ideals. Alexandra quotes from his private diary the following passage:

If I heard about myself from the outside, as of a person, living in luxury, with police guards, grabbing all he could from the peasants, putting them in the lockup, and professing and preaching Christianity, and handing out small coins, and hiding behind a sweet wife while I did all these base things—I could not but call him a scoundrel! And that is what I have had to submit to, so that I could free myself from human fame and live for the sake of my soul. (*Tolstoy: A Life of My Father*, 1953, 466)

On another occasion, he writes, "Help me, O Lord. Again I yearn to go away, and I dare not. Nor can I give up." These passages demonstrate the extent to which he fought for years with the dilemmas of his own existence, seeking resolution, some way out and forward. His inheriting great wealth and position became for him a burden and contradiction of the sincerity of his religious beliefs, as they developed and evolved, and weighed heavily upon him. Eventually, seeking to free himself, he legally passed ownership of his estate and holdings to Sophia and the family. All his religious writings, several books and many pamphlets, plays, and short stories can be properly understood only when approached in the light of this struggle. It explains why he lived in such a simple way that many visitors to Yasnaya Polyana recorded their surprise upon actually meeting him and witnessing it for themselves. The only solution for Tolstoy was what it was and is for all great writers. He had to write his way through his dilemmas, create for himself the role and persona that resolved his deepest conflicts, and those of his time. That is what all the religious works are about. By the end of his last decade, he's achieved it, and then, finally, he's ready, to follow the way of the ancients, set an example, remind the world, in deed as well as word, of the spiritual journey of life, round out the fullness of his own life.

By Tolstoy's own testimony, after the years of happiness with Sophia, after writing his early novels and stories, including *War and Peace* and most of *Anna Karenina*, he experienced a searing spiritual crisis, feeling his life had become meaningless, which impelled him on a search for meaning and purpose. As recounted in *My Confessions* (1878), during his early years prior to his marriage, he states,

I killed people in war and challenged to duels to kill; I lost money at cards, wasting the labour of the peasants; I punished them, fornicated, and cheated. Lying, stealing, acts of lust of every description, drunkenness, violence, murder—There was not a crime which I did not commit, and for all that I was praised, and my contemporaries have regarded me as a comparatively moral man.

He further emphasizes that he reached a point where "life had no meaning at all." Overwhelmed by the emptiness of his existence, he turned to the study of philosophy, but eventually came to believe that there must be more than reason:

From the beginning of the human race, wherever there is life, there is the faith which makes life possible and everywhere the leading characteristics of that faith are the same.

From his study of Buddhism, Islam, and Christianity, as early as 1879, Tolstoy arrives at the understanding that he is "a part of the infinite whole" and in "the answers given by faith was to be found the deepest source of human wisdom," while rejecting "the unnecessary and unreasonable doctrines" that had crept into all of the great religions. Initially, he returns to the Russian Orthodox Church, but soon finds it suffered from many irrational doctrines, what he would call after his 1901 excommunication "sorcery," leading to his quest for the truth of Christianity, and all religions, that lasted until the end of his life in 1910.

A hundred years later, part of the difficulty many people may have in understanding Tolstoy involves today the pervasive nihilism of the academic and cultural establishment, which since Tolstoy's death, has continued to drain away all spiritual import and nuance, not merely from Tolstoy's work, but from literature and life. Western civilization itself has become suffused with nihilism, identified with it, the ruling

24

Enlightenment myth celebrated everywhere has become the ascendance and triumphalism of a gloriously secular nihilism, passing the disease around the world, to all countries and cultures, so that the remedy can now only be found and administered in a truly global context. Far beyond the confines of the literary, intellectual, academic milieu, East or West, the ethos of nihilism, inculcated into the young and the educated culture, pervades, in its local variants, every region of the globe. Tolstoy himself was highly aware that the general direction of culture was set in a direction away from religious belief and understood his efforts as a response to it, as when he said of Nietzsche, "What savagery! It is terrible, so to drag down Christianity!" Similarly, Tolstoy rejected the applicability of a solely materialistic understanding of the human being, whether by Marx or Thomas Henry Huxley's crude distortions of Charles Darwin in his Romanes Lectures of 1894. Tolstoy states, "the law of evolution runs counter to the moral law: This was known to the ancient Greeks and Hindus. The philosophy and religion of both those peoples brought them to the doctrine of self-renunciation." It was often against the decline of a spiritual and moral understanding of the human being that Tolstoy understood himself as writing and working, though even he underestimated the force of nihilism as manifested in 1917. In a preface to Tolstoy's short novels, the literary critic and editor of *Partisan Review*, Philip Rahv, observed, "Tolstoy resisted the catastrophic ruin of the traditional order by straining all the powers of his reason to discover a way out." Tolstoy used not only his reason but the power of his soul.

As recorded in an often-cited journal entry, the idea had already occurred to Tolstoy when he was twenty-seven years old that the world needed a new religion, one purged of the false doctrines of organized Christianity:

A new religion corresponding with the present state of mankind; the religion of Christ but purged of dogmas and mysticism—a practical religion, not promising future bliss but giving bliss on earth.

After his religious crisis, as early as 1884, he took note of his intention of compiling the sayings of religious sages and thinkers into a single volume. During the last decade of his life, he finally began the compilation in earnest, resulting in several different versions of it, variously titled, *Thoughts of Wise Men*, *A Calendar of Wisdom*, *A Circle of Reading*, with the final edition in 1910, *The Path of Life*. Tolstoy spent much of his energy on the book, compiling and refining. He himself considered it as the most important work of his life, as he once wrote, "If it is granted me to finish this work, it will be a complete statement of my world outlook." He continually simplified and revised the quotations and passages to the point that he advised translators not to look for the original pieces in Confucius, Buddhism, or wherever, but to base their translations on his own free-renderings. Near the end of his life, far ahead of his time, he couldn't understand why people didn't use *The Circle of Reading* more. While he understood that a writer cannot create his own religion, he was caught in the dilemma of finding all the existing forms unfulfilling.

Throughout the last thirty years of his life, Tolstoy was opposed to the violence in Russia advanced by the radicals, Marxists, and socialists of his time. In a journal entry he writes,

> Socialists will never destroy poverty and the injustice of the inequality of capacities. The strongest and more intelligent will always make use of the weaker and the more stupid. Justice and equality in the good things of life will never be achieved by anything less than Christianity, i.e., by negating oneself and recognizing the meaning of one's life in service to others.

His background in and experience of the ruling aristocratic class and ethos provided Tolstoy with an acute understanding of power and its endless corruptions. Far from being naive about power in society, he understood that human beings had to have a change of heart to influence society at the deepest level. The bombs and bullets of the revolutionaries were anathema to him and would produce only another tyranny, as they indeed did, one of the most horrible and blood-thirsty tyrannies in the history of humanity. Elsewhere, Tolstoy observed, "The object of socialism is the satisfaction of the lowest needs of man: his material well being. And it cannot attain even this end by the means it recommends." Similarly, in "An Appeal," "Even if that should happen which Marx predicted, then the only thing that will happen is that despotism will be passed on. Now the capitalists are ruling, but then the directors of the working class will rule." In 1905 in "The End of the Age," he wrote, "Nothing demonstrates so clearly the increasing enslavement of nations as the growth, spread, and success of socialistic theories." By the last decade of his life, he had long since concluded that only a deep spiritual change could truly ameliorate the condition of humanity.

Arguing always against the violence of socialism and the Marxists, Tolstoy, unfortunately, interpreted the New Testament in such a way that non-resistance to violence prevented him from being sufficiently practical enough to recognize the value of a more democratic order, causing him to advocate a type of Christian anarchism and to repudiate Russian efforts to create a democratic body, the Duma, in the early years of the twentieth century. He also, unfortunately, aligned himself with much of the thinking of the anarchist Peter Kropotkin and the anti-tax thinker Henry George. Like Dostoyevsky, he really didn't understand the West. As others have remarked, a few trips to Europe and England failed to take him deep enough into the social and political culture. Both he and Dostoevsky were too quick to resort to Catholicism as a whipping boy to explain every flaw of the West. Yet I cannot but feel, given the subsequently bloody Soviet history, the country and people would have been better off had Tolstoy been more moderate and realistic about the necessities of life and government. Still, the Christian anarchism of Tolstoy was infinitely more gentle than what Lenin instituted in 1917. In the end, Russia has come full circle back to most of the issues that Tolstoy struggled with, as has the 21st Century.

Tolstoy significantly located what he believed the only way forward in universality—the recognition that the human being is a spiritual being, grounded in the necessity of moral choice and growth toward perfection, as in all the great religions. Our global, pluralistic age lives this truth even as it fails sufficiently to recognize and articulate it to the level required to help understand the nature of life in our time. Perhaps more than any other piece he wrote, published in 1902, Tolstoy explains the religious philosophy he came to hold in *What Is Religion, and Wherein Lies Its Essence?*

> Religions differ in their external forms, but they are all alike in their fundamental principles. And it is these principles, that are fundamental to all religions, that form the true religion which alone at the present time is suitable for us all, and the adoption of which alone can save men from their ills….

Having by this time written several major books and numerous articles on religion, struggling with Christian history and doctrine, his own excommunication in 1901 by the Orthodox Church, Tolstoy was uniquely qualified by fiery experience and study to set forth his increasingly universal beliefs:

> The principles of this true religion are so natural to men, that as soon as they are put before them they are accepted as something quite familiar and self-evident. For us the true religion is Christianity in those of its principles in which it agrees, not with the external forms, but with the basic principles of Brahmanism, Confucianism, Taoism, Hebraism, Buddhism, and even Mohammedanism. And

just in the same way, for those who profess Brahmanism, Confucianism, etc.—true religion is that of which the basic principles agree with those of all other religions. And these principles are very simple, intelligible and clear.

In this sense, referring to the thinking of Tolstoy, as is often done, as Christian anarchism is a distortion of what the man really believed—spiritual universality, or Christianity universalized, might be better terms, represented best by the same universal spirit he labored to articulate in *A Calendar of Wisdom* (tr. Peter Sekirin, 1997). Tolstoy was so far ahead of his time people failed to understand the universality that he was struggling to find and express.

Defining universally held principles, in *What Is Religion*..., he states,

These principles are that there is a God, the origin of all things; that in man dwells a spark from that Divine Origin, which man, by his way of living, can increase or decrease in himself; that to increase this divine spark man must suppress his passions and increase love in himself; and that the practical means to attain this result is to do to others as you would they should do to you. All these principles are common to Brahmanism, Hebraism, Confucianism, and Mohammedanism. (If Buddhism supplies no definition of God, it nevertheless acknowledges That with which man commingles, and into Which he is absorbed when he attains to Nirvana. So, That with which man commingles, or into Which he is absorbed in Nirvana, is the same Origin that is called God in Hebraism, Christianity, and Mohammedanism.)

Repeatedly and everywhere in Tolstoy's writing, clearing away the debris of such ephemera as anarchism, one finds his emphasis on the Golden Rule as the essential teaching of all wisdom traditions and religions. Just as lucidly and consistently,

Tolstoy understood the importance of reason and that true religion does not subvert it to "sorcery" and other irrationalities:

> Religion is not a belief, settled once for all, in certain supernatural occurrences supposed to have taken place once upon a time, nor in the necessity for certain prayers and ceremonies; nor is it, as the scientists suppose, a survival of the superstitions of ancient ignorance, which in our time has no meaning or application to life; but religion is a certain relation of man to eternal life and to God, a relation accordant with reason and contemporary knowledge, and it is the one thing that alone moves humanity forward towards its destined aim.

Tolstoy utterly opposed the caricatures of faith and religion by modern Scientism, believing as Ernest J. Simmons remarked that "one of the main calamities of modern life" was "the tendency to replace moral and spiritual progress by technical progress." His trust in and search for rational truth enabled him to see through both the irrationalities and blind-faith of organized religion and Scientism to the universality of the human spirit. He was, in a sense, an early modern seeker of the spiritual unity of the great religions, preceding and akin to the Perennial Philosophy of Aldous Huxley and others, but less given to the esoteric, closer to the approach of Huston Smith and Joseph Campbell, superior even to them, I would say, though admittedly their gifts are different.

When I think of Tolstoy's spiritual journey and of earlier times and cultures, of writers struggling with what is universal in the human being, I think of Dara Shikoh in Mughal India, seeking the unity of Hinduism and Islam, as in his *The Mingling of the Two Oceans* (1657), the universality of the Sufi poets, or of the Dali Lama's recent book *Toward a True Kinship of Faiths: How the World's Religions Can Come Together* (2010). As reported by Tolstoy's daughter Alexandra, almost his last gasping words were "To seek, always to seek." In the sense of the psychiatrist Viktor Frankl in his book *Man's Search for Meaning*, he was one who never ceased searching for truth. Far from a religious organization and all that that implies, Tolstoy conceived of religious belief in rational, reasonable terms, opposed to organized Christianity, as when he wrote, "Men of our modern world who profess this perverted form of Christianity really believe in nothing at all. And that is the peculiar character of our time." That is why he relentlessly argued against the distortions that he believed had come to exist in the doctrines of institutional Christianity, in favor of a more humanistic, open conception of faith. In "The End of the World," putting aside "false Christianity," Tolstoy looked forward to "true Christianity," one freed from "sorcery," universal in scope and outlook:

> I think that at present—at this very time—the life of the Christian nations is near to the limit dividing the old epoch which is ending from the new which is beginning. I think that now at this very time that great revolution has begun which for almost 2000 years has been preparing in all Christendom; a revolution consisting in the replacing of false Christianity and the consequent power of one portion of mankind and the slavery of another—by true Christianity and the consequent recognition of that equality and true liberty which are natural to all rational beings.

All the more reason why the caricatures of Tolstoy in "The Last Station" and A. N. Wilson's biography, as in the biographies of Alexander Boot (2009), and Rosamund Bartlett (2011), jarred so incongruously against my understanding of who the man actually was, in and of himself, as articulated in his own writings, over the entire last half of his life, especially the last decade. It was also the real Tolstoy who meant so much to Gandhi, the one who emphasized spirituality, love, peace, and non-resistance to evil. "His secret is that he is the last of the unalienated artists," Philip Rahv insightfully observed. Similarly, Saul Bellow remarked on the extent to which Tolstoy was "healthy," far from the "adversarial" writers of Lionel Trilling.

Now more than ever, after centuries of falling down into the bottomless pit of nihilism, the world needs to recover the vision of universality, what the great religions and people of the various countries and cultures have in common. For all too long, humanity has been obsessed with what distinguishes and separates, what divides people from one another, setting up our little racial, nationalistic gods and idols. Tolstoy was interested in what we have in common, what unifies our vision, hoping thereby to elevate and improve, to whatever degree possible, our actions. It is long past time that the world re-affirm human unity. Tolstoy provides a significant part of the perspective required to achieve it.

Alexandra reports in her book *Tolstoy: A Life of My Father* (1953) that he had a visitor in February of 1909 who was a Bahai, a member of a faith that emphasizes what is universal in all religions:

> "Actually, when you think of it," Father said, "you are always astonished that such a simple argument does not come to your mind. Take an Orthodox Christian, a Catholic, a Buddhist—all of them believing in what they hold to be the truth. Yet if I cross a certain boundary—I think that the one is a lie, the other the truth. What doubts that arouses, what need to search out the religion which would be common to all!" (472)

Alexandra continues that her father had worked unrelentingly on *The Circle of Reading* precisely because he was seeking "what was basic to all religions," trying "to lay the foundation for one religion." It is important to stress that the Bahai faith that Tolstoy responded to was not what is known to many people today as the Baha'i Faith, the highly organized, would-be theocracy located in Haifa, Israel, merely one of several Bahai denominations, which has become exactly the kind of exclusive religious organization that Tolstoy vehemently condemned in all his writings. Rather, Tolstoy responded to the open and inclusive association and movement that existed under Abdul-Baha, the son of the founder of the Bahai faith, Baha'u'llah, who died in 1892 in present-day Israel. Until his own death in 1921, Abdul-Baha brought his father's vision into the Western, modern world, showing the way beyond its Islamic and Sufi heritage, emphasizing universality, "spiritual democracy," the "oneness of religion," and the freedom of the individual soul in self-less love and service to humanity, as in other persuasions. Tolstoy's papers establish that as early as 1894, he had heard of the Bahai movement, which traces its origin to 1863, with many Bahai contacts extending until the end of his life, including his receipt of books, letters, articles, and visitors familiar with the Bahai teachings, along with the droves of other people visiting Yasnaya Polyana. Reported by Tolstoy's personal physician, Dushan Makovitsky, in his diary, for May 15, 1910, Tolstoy observed in his presence that the Bahai movement was "Very profound. I know of no other so profound" (Vol. 4, 255). Honesty makes it incumbent on all trying to enlist him under their banner to recognize as well that Tolstoy is on record as writing, "I know the Bahai Teachings, and I am in agreement with its basic principles, except for the belief in the infallibility of its founders, and a few other details" (Polnoe Sobranie Sochinenii, Vol 81, 77).

Many people today still commonly think in terms of "your" religion, and "my" religion, as in "the" religion, "the" exclusive truth, while the deepest meaning of universality is "our" religion, not, to be clear, even "my" own *personal* Bahai persuasion, not defined as a "box," which is but one form of universality, conceived of as neutral territory, or "yours," whether any type of transcendence, atheism, nihilism or whatever. Universality embraces all persuasions and transcends them. That is its great challenge. And it is not relativism. The tendency always is to think of religion in terms of organized or institutional religion, which isn't religion at all. True religion can only be personal, and as pluralistic as the Golden Rule. Take the person out of it and it is no longer religion. In the modern world, even throughout human history, true religion has never been organized. It is not the nature of spirituality to take over and dominate the communal, collective space. And it definitely can not ever be organized. For it is, as Tolstoy understood so well, about the individual soul and his or her inmost relation to the Divine. The astonishing development of religious history, I want to say revelation, is that it is the Will of God that religion not be organized.

Everywhere people are against organized religion for countless good reasons, as was Tolstoy. He and most people, if interested in religion, not the falsities and sophistries of exclusive institutional doctrine, want the true thing of the heart. That doesn't mean oppressively organized religion, anathema to the soul. Religion-become-doctrine disperses the mystery from lived life. I attended once an interfaith meeting in which two Christian ministers spent much of the time rehashing consubstantiation versus transubstantiation in front of Muslims, Sikhs, Hindus, and others, as to which interpretation was essentially the "true" Christianity. I've never been able to see any Christianity in either, and I'm someone who actually studied those doctrines, at various times in my life, out of historical and literary interest. Much of the culture is frozen in all those antiquated categories of "religion," and then much of the rest of it is locked into fighting against those outdated conceptions, believing it's defending "The Enlightenment" when it is just as misguided and outdated in its own way as Christian fundamentalists, skewing its own thinking, while our crises loom ever larger.

The deepest insight of human experience remains, "Truth is One; sages call it by many names." The Divine Being transcends all human conceptions. We truly need every human attempt to understand Him, Her, It, yet even then, in all humility, have the dimmest hope of fully understanding. It is precisely the defense-reaction of the cynicism of modernity, as Viktor Frankl insightfully observes, that rejects the meaningfulness of life, believing all religions are false, delusional, contemptible fantasies. From Freud, Marx, sundry sociologists and many others, science debased to the substitute religion of Scientism, the verdict and message is almost invariably condescension and contempt. As Julien Benda observed in *The Betrayal of the Clerks* (1927), modernity derides any spiritual vision, including Tolstoy's. Benda, though, remained limited by the exclusivism of his own Catholic universalism, a limited form of universality. Far from such a limitation, Tolstoy arrived at the last station of modernity, universality, long before he arrived at the station of Astapovo, long before the rest of humanity began to catch up. Though we may still first blow up much of the world, or poison it with radiation, as at Chernobyl and Fukushima, global modernity is increasingly catching up with Tolstoy, however unknowingly, pulling into the last station of humanity.

Leo Tolstoy's *Hadji Murad*

In 2009 I downloaded and read from Google Books Tolstoy's novella *Hadji Murad*. It's one of the last pieces of fiction he wrote, finishing it in 1904, published in 1911, a year after his death. The short novel, about two-hundred pages on an ereader, has always been praised as an exquisitely crafted work of art. Tolstoy allows the structure and interplay of events to speak for themselves, eschewing nearly all temptation to explain to the reader his intentions and meaning. For precisely this reason, the book may be an especially challenging one. Before stating what I think of *Hadji Murad*, I must touch again on my very long relationship with Tolstoy.

As a young undergraduate at Eastern Michigan University in 1976, I used to read Tolstoy when I was supposed to be studying "more important" things. I would go to the library and comb through the many feet of his *Collected Works*, devouring many of the more obscure, less-read books by him. While taking classes in Shakespeare, Chaucer, and the romantic poets, I reveled in his works *What Is Art?*, "Essay on Shakespeare," and *The Kingdom of God Is Within You*. I well realized these works were anathema to most of the ruling academic establishment, whom I was beginning to realize even as far back as then were sunk in doctrinaire nihilism. I thrilled to read a writer who believed literature could and should have a spiritual dimension, as do our lives, if we are at all awake and sensitive to the Divine.

From, *What is Art?*:

> Special importance has always been given by all men to that...which transmits feelings flowing from their religious perception, and this small part of art they have specifically called art, attaching to it the full meaning of the word. That was how men of old—Socrates, Plato, and Aristotle—looked on art. Thus did the Hebrew prophets and the ancient Christians regard art; thus it was, and still

is, understood by the Mahommedans, and thus is it still understood by religious folk among our own peasantry.

The business of art lies just in this—to make that understood and felt which, in the form of an argument, might be incomprehensible and inaccessible. Usually it seems to the recipient of a truly artistic impression that he knew the thing before but had been unable to express it.

Art is the transmission of feelings flowing from man's religious perception.

So that good, great, universal, religious art may be incomprehensible to a small circle of spoilt people, but certainly not to any large number of plain men.

How excited I was to discover Google Books now has available online all that huge stretch of library shelf devoted to Tolstoy. I eagerly downloaded all of it, including *Hadji Murad*, which I have thought of for years, sensing there was something in the book I needed to read, at the right time, now come, one of Tolstoy's last artistic communications to the world.

As a young man Tolstoy had served in the Russian military in the Caucasus and in Crimea. His early stories and books reflect such experience. Late in life, he found himself recalling that time in the 1850s, while walking through a newly ploughed field in 1896, noticing a beautiful thistle that had been bent and broken by the plough. He tried to save it, but couldn't, it was so damaged. The incident became a metaphor evoking the life of a local fighter Tolstoy had actually met, Hadji Murad, who was caught between the fanaticism of an Islamic war-lord named Shamil, who was intent on taking over Chechnya, and the Russians, who were extending their control into the area. Hadji Murad, as a man belonging to the more peaceful, local Sufi-like branch of Islam, known as Muridism, resisted the onslaught of Shamil's jihad and fundamentalist fanaticism. Hoping to obtain troops from the Russians with which to fight off Shamil, Murad leads his band of men over to the Russians, ultimately being caught between the opposing forces. Tolstoy's art lies in what he makes of and does with these facts of history. His perceiving sensibility and interpretation is subtle and attuned to the issues on all sides.

In the end, the Russians fail to provide Hadji Murad with the troops he needs to protect the Murid community from dominance by Shamil's fanatics. He waits and waits while the incompetent and corrupt Russian political machine misunderstands what is involved and bungles the chance Murad has offered it. Tolstoy is especially insightful and scathing on the moral and spiritual corruption of the Russian elite and monarchy, contrasting its decline with the healthier vitality of Hadji Murad's village simplicity, spiritual vigor, and self-less service to his community. Tolstoy's art fully critiques both Western Christianity and the Islam of beheadings and the chopping off of hands. Murad's values and beliefs, pure, unsullied, grounded in mystical prayer and communion, are crushed between the two. Finally despairing of Russian help, especially in time to rescue his own family, rendered pawns in Shamil's intrigues, Murad decides to make a break from Russian confinement to save his family, an act misinterpreted by the Russian garrison which sends troops out after him, murdering his men and beheading him, no better than Shamil's tactics. Tolstoy's tragedy of *Hadji Murad* resonates with the accents of art and vision, challenging the reader to understand.

It seems to me, though, that few have understood. For instance, Harold Bloom's discussion of *Hadji Murad* overemphasizes the tragedy while neglecting the Islamic, Sufi resonance. It may be that Bloom's Jewish loyalties led to his misreading the book. Perhaps we have a larger context today in which we can begin to perceive the profundity of Tolstoy's art, what with the collapse of Utopia in Power and the terrorism of 9/11. I often think the world has not really come to grips with the implications of 9/11. The various traumatized dualisms of perspective that have become common, though understandable, fail to seek out sufficiently the spiritual dimensions from a wide enough view, or deep enough. I feel it calls into question what humanity has become, how we conceive of ourselves, the purpose of life, the meaning of all our traditions of religious and spiritual guidance and wisdom, as well as secular assumptions. The world spins on, we're still in our old boxes, desperately in need of a new vision, victims as well as terrorists and fundamentalists. To me, the real battle is spiritual. Not often said or allowed on the evening news or in the other ossified sectors of modern culture. Despite some of his cranky personal flaws, mostly the result of his support of the anarchist Kropotkin, and so on, Tolstoy was an astonishing artist of incredible vision and foresight, part of the tragedy of his time.

The Poet's Religion of Rabindranath Tagore

I cannot write about Tagore without writing about what he has meant to me as a poet during the course of more than forty years of reading him. In the early 1970s he became for me a model and mentor, an example of the poet's life, one which resonated deeply with my own experience, especially in spiritual terms, which I eventually learned was taboo even to mention in the learned halls of American universities, where God was and is usually dead, and no one desiring intellectual respectability had better utter the slightest syllable otherwise. To write about Tagore also requires that I mention Robert Frost, for they came together in my mind, however incongruous it may seem, to represent a tradition of independent and spiritual search for truth and knowledge that only a poet of genuine calling can exemplify. Having read in high school, in a world religion class, *The World Bible*, a classic collection of religious scriptures from all the great faiths, including Hinduism, with extracts from the Upanishads, I was open to what Tagore had to teach. The American tradition that Robert Frost represents, of the poet going off on his own to find himself and write, spoke deeply to me, as did his words that "it might be necessary…to stay away from school or at least play hooky a good deal to season slowly out of doors." That had already been my life and experience. In Tagore's address in Calcutta regarding the Nobel Prize, I found essentially the idea of what I was doing, though with Frost primarily in mind. Tagore's early years on his houseboat tending to his family's estate, left largely alone, as he relates, to reflect and develop as a poet, spoke deeply to me as did his poems in his book *Gitanjali*. Reading Tagore, Whitman, Hafez, and Rumi, living on an old farm in Oakland Township, Michigan, near where I had grown up in Rochester, I knew it was right to trust the Muse, the promptings of my heart that told me that I would not find what I needed as a poet in the university, but only through independent struggle and search, by study of the masters of the art. Whether East or West, the poets I admired set the arduous example. I couldn't explain it to my family and friends, but I couldn't deny what I felt inside. Tagore helped give me the strength to follow the Man of my Heart.

It was in Tagore's *Reminiscences* that I found early on the confirmation of my own experience of transcendence. Writing of his "awakening" at a house rented by his brother on Sudder Street in Calcutta, Tagore relates that "a momentous revolution of some kind came about within me." Pacing the balcony at sunset, he experienced an overwhelming sense of the obliteration of self, filling him with "beauty and joy," "seeing the world in its own true aspect." Then for a second time he experienced it during sunrise, "all of a sudden a covering seemed to fall away from my eyes, and I found the world bathed in a wonderful radiance, with waves of beauty and joy swelling on every side." I had had similar experiences of transcendence and joy, in my early twenties, once standing in a line in a mundane supermarket, an ordinary setting, during which I was suddenly swept up into a feeling of love and unity with all the diverse people around me, housewives and children, people of various races and backgrounds, attending to the simple necessities of life. Love for all humanity rolled over me lifting me into a state of indescribable bliss. No one around me knew what I had just experienced but it changed my life forever. Not all the nihilism and cynicism of modernity could gainsay the authenticity of what I had been allowed to experience. Tagore further strengthened and fortified my trust and understanding in what I had been through, what it meant, helping me to find a way forward on my solitary journey.

To understand Tagore, it is necessary to make an effort, at least to some degree, to understand the social and family background that produced him. Tagore often acknowledged he was indebted to Rammohan Roy, an early reformer of Hinduism in the late 18th and 19th centuries, often called the father of modern India, as by Krishna Kripalani in his outstanding monograph on Roy. As a young boy, Roy had had an excellent education in Arabic and Persian, along with study of Islam, and then Sanskrit and the traditional texts of the Upanishads, followed later by time in Tibet studying Buddhism, all of which led to his realizing the essential unity of the great religions, that they all taught the oneness of the Supreme Being and the unity of humanity, emphasizing basic moral and ethical virtue. He repeatedly created space for people of similar mind and persuasion to meet to discuss and worship together, among whom was Tagore's grandfather Dwarkanath Tagore. As early as 1823, Rammohan Roy was in communication with Christian Unitarian missionaries in Calcutta, frequently attending their services. Simplifying a complicated history, in 1830 he was the founder of the Brahmo Sabha for the Worship of the One True God, a trust which increasingly became a reform movement in the next generation. Often alone in his struggle to help his fellow Brahmins and countrymen, Roy argued that the Upanishads had a highly monotheistic conception of deity and asserted that many innovations and corrupt teachings had crept into the everyday practice of Brahminism.

The next generation produced a gifted new leader in the person of Tagore's own father, Debendranath Tagore, a man noted for his genuine spiritual qualities, referred to as Maharshi or "saint," and who eventually transformed Roy's group of mostly friends into the Brahmo Samaj, making it a widespread national movement in 1843 with a number of houses of worship scattered around the country. The poet, Rabindranath Tagore, was born in 1861, at a time when the Brahmo Samaj was transitioning partly to new leadership and was himself eventually appointed by his father as a secretary to the organization as a young man in 1884, leading to his writing about Rammohan Roy on a number of occasions. There occasionally continued to be contact and exchange between some Unitarians and members of the Brahmo Samaj; one of its leaders visited the United States and spoke at Unitarian meetings in the 1880s. Rabindranath was born and raised under the close guidance of his father and this spiritual tradition suffused the Tagore home and family, instilling in him a lasting respect and love for the teachings of the Upanishads.

Recalling his father in his *Reminiscences*, which was written in 1912, Tagore mentions being awakened to recite Sanskrit prayers with him and visiting the Sikh Golden Temple in Amritsar, chanting with devotees songs of devotion on the island in the lake. He also relates singing songs in the streets with itinerant religious singers while visiting the Himalayas with his father in 1884. By 1910 he had already written many books in several genres and had spent much of the years since 1905 involved in public and political controversies. Following his wife's death in 1902, he had also lost his father and two of his children. Yet as a poet he had struggled and written his way through pain and suffering, writing many of the poems that were to become part of his book *Gitanjali*, which was to win him worldwide recognition through the Nobel Prize for Literature. At this point in his life, in 1910, he wrote an essay entitled "My Religion," a piece perhaps now relatively obscure in the West, judging by the fact that I had to have a copy taken out of storage to get my hands on it. The essay foreshadows the various collections that were to come that muse and meditate on the meaning of life in his unique blend of the teachings of the Upanishads, the Brahmo Samaj, Baul poets and other religious singers and seers of India, all of which undergird his poetry and literary writing. Right at the outset Tagore makes it clear that he is not talking about a doctrinal, organized religion of tight little creeds and dogmas, sweeping aside outward "religion":

Man possesses an extra awareness that is greater than his material sense—this is his manhood. It is this deep-abiding creative force which is his religion. So that in my language the word 'religion' has a profound meaning. The 'wateriness' of water is essentially its religion, in the spark of the flame lies the religion of fire. Likewise, Man's religion is his innermost truth.

In man—in every human being—truth abides in its

universal form, and alongside it has also its individual aspect. Herein lies one's own special religion. It is here that man recognises the variedness of the universe. From the standpoint of creation this variedness is a valuable thing. That is why we are not endowed with a power that can totally destroy it *(A Tagore Testament*, 1953).

Most people regard a "communal term" as religion, "Christian," "Mohammedan," "Vaishnava," and so on, such boxes mistaken for the inner reality of the "universal form." In actuality, the "inner heart knows" a distinctive relationship "reigns supreme," giving a "special delight" or joy, which it alone experiences and expresses through its individual personality, both on the mundane and higher levels, far beyond ordinary "religion." As Tagore says, "Man's religion is his innermost truth." Exterior religion by definition has got it wrong. In his own way, to essentialize, admittedly, in a sense, Tagore struggled and wrote against the tide of orthodox Hinduism, its rites, rituals, and multiplicity of idols and gods. For Tagore, God was One, the Brahma of the Upanishads, the Supreme Person, the Infinite Being beyond all human conceptions, redolent of the mystics and seers of the ancient forest hermitages and Mughal India.

Focusing on a crucial part of all this, Tagore writes that if man's "achievement in the outer world" fails to coincide with "his inner truth," "it creates a rupture in his very existence." The "inner truth" must also find its place or articulation in the outer world. There must be an appropriate resonance. Man does not exist "only within himself." Insightfully, Tagore continues, "he also exists a great deal through others by the way he is known to them," "a vital necessity." The "inner awareness" of man must find expression and reflection in and through the social milieu, through connection with fellow human beings. The "true nature" of one's "own religion" does not constitute solipsism or narcissism, for it is not "totally confined within me." Its "creative force" finds outlets in "various ways," consciously and unconsciously, making its presence felt. This has been my life-long battle as a poet and writer, having in my early twenties, forty years ago, become a member of an outer religion that I thought was congruent with my inner religion. I have had to take a long journey, even to the moon, to realize the truth of what Tagore meant and to realize that in its most universal form faith transcends its own exterior self and definitions in favor of the inner one. Tagore often suggested the mystics in all the great traditions made such a journey.

In the years before writing "My Religion," Tagore had given it form in his poetry, as in this poem, translated by Tagore himself, from *Naivedya*, "Offering" (1901):

Far as I gaze at the depth of Thy immensity
I find no trace there of sorrow or death or separation.
Death assumes its aspect of terror
and sorrow its pain
only when, away from Thee,
I turn my face toward my own dark self.
Thou All Perfect,
everything abides at Thy feet
for all time.
The fear of loss only clings to me
with its ceaseless grief,
but the shame of my penury
and my life's burden
vanish in a moment
when I feel Thy presence
in the center of my being.

The speaker finds "inner truth" "in the center of my being," feeling "Thy presence" in the deepest recesses of the heart, where no traces of "sorrow or death or separation" can reach, the "All Perfect" resolving such travails and disruptions of one's "own dark self." A number of the poems in *Naivedya* appear in the English *Gitanjali* and significantly shape the perception of Tagore as a mystic poet and writer, although in his stories and other writing he has also had other social concerns, largely unknown to many readers in the West. I believe it is fair to say, though, that the West did not create such an image of Tagore. It is clearly his own self-definition and conception of who and what he was and remains evinced in his books and writings. Always an immensely prolific writer, his many books after *Gitanjali* continue predominantly in this vein. The revisionist notion that the West created "Hinduism" is just as false when applied to Tagore.

In October of 1912, Tagore visited the United States where his son was completing a graduate degree in agriculture at the University of Illinois in Champaign-Urbana. While there for some months, Tagore was invited by Albert Vail, a Unitarian minister, to speak repeatedly at his church.[1] As the scholar Krishna Kripalani states in his excellent biography of Tagore, he eventually wrote several lectures and "later delivered them at Harvard University and other places," publishing them in 1913 as *Sadhana: The Realisation of Life*. In it Tagore mentions that he was "brought up in a family where texts of the Upanishads are used in daily worship" and that "Western readers will have the opportunity of coming into touch with the ancient spirit of India." He states all the great religious traditions "have to be judged not by the letter but by the spirit" and are of "living importance," not dead artifacts in a museum. In the ancient forest hermitages, India had evolved "the early ideal of strenuous self-realisation," putting all her emphasis on "the harmony that exists between the individual and the universe." Highlighting an important tenet and practice, Tagore states,

> Thus the text of our everyday meditation is the Gayatri, a verse which is considered to be the epitome of all the

---

[1]Albert Vail eventually calls for a "universal synthesis" of the great religions in his 1970 book *Transforming Light: The Living Heritage of World Religions*. Harper & Row.

Vedas. By its help we try to realise the essential unity of the world with the conscious soul of man; we learn to perceive the unity held together by the one Eternal Spirit, whose power creates the earth, the sky, and the stars, and at the same time irradiates our minds with the light of a consciousness that moves and exists in unbroken continuity with the outer world.

Krishna Kripalani explains that "the Gayatri remained his lifelong companion for Tagore and he continued to find in it a source of strength and joy long after he had discarded the sacred thread" (47). As a young boy Tagore had learnt and meditated on the Gayatri, and, judging by his own comments, it suffused his outlook and conception of life. While Tagore inevitably evolved with modern Indian culture away from the more rigid forms of Brahmism, as instanced by his relinquishing the sacred thread which he was entitled to wear by birth as a member of the Brahmin class, the integrity of his interior spiritual beliefs appear very consistent across the length of his lifetime. The rest of *Sadhana* traces the "realisation" of "the essential unity of the world with the conscious soul of man" through various levels of consciousness and in terms of action, beauty, and the infinite. Yet Tagore draws on not only the Upanishads in his discussion but also Buddhism and Christianity, and includes a surprisingly wide-ranging engagement with modern science for a writer of the time, East or West. Tagore's consciousness embraces much that is beyond the confines of traditional Brahminism, and however one might choose to define Sanatana Dharma, the "Eternal Law." He's clearly moving into an ever-increasing universality, even more than he may have realized.

I find particularly striking his reflections on dharma, defining it as "the ultimate purpose that is working in our self," like a seed bearing a tree within. "Only when the tree begins to take shape do you come to see its dharma." Elaborating, Tagore writes,

When we know the highest ideal of freedom [perhaps mukti] which a man has, we know his dharma, the essence of his nature, the real meaning of his self. At first sight it seems that man counts that as freedom by which he gets unbounded opportunities of self-gratification and self-aggrandisement. But surely this is not borne out by history. Our revelatory men have always been those who have lived the life of self-sacrifice. The higher nature in man always seeks for something which transcends itself and yet is its deepest truth; which claims all its sacrifice, yet makes this sacrifice its own recompense. This is man's dharma, man's religion, and man's self is the vessel which is to carry this sacrifice to the altar.

He further suggests about sacrifice, by analogy, that the lamp must give up its oil to produce its light, for the good of others, out of love, as Buddha had taught. Thereby, the lamp finds the purpose and meaning of its existence, through selfless service finding joy. Tagore expands on all this in terms of the Bhagavad Gita and the Upanishads, exploring the fact that sacrifice is one of the great truths and mysteries of human existence. The personal sacrifice that Tagore must have constantly been called upon to accept in order to write the flood of works that he unrelentingly poured out must have been of almost inconceivable proportions. It may very well have been that only through daily prayer and meditation was it possible to find the necessary peace of mind, composure, strength, and submission to carry on.

While Tagore wrote and delivered the chapters of *Sadhana* as sermons or addresses, the *Gitanjali* was in press in London, coming out in November of 1912.

Ever in my life have I sought thee with my songs. It was they who led me from door to door, and with them have I felt about me, searching and touching my world.

It was my songs that taught me all the lessons I ever learnt; they showed me secret paths, they brought before my sight many a star on the horizon of my heart.

They guided me all the daylong to the mysteries of the country of pleasure and pain, and, at last, to what palace gate have they brought me in the evening at the end of my journey?

The dharma of the poet manifests itself through his poems, their unfolding guidance taking him as by the hand, leading a little boy homeward, "searching and touching" his world, carrying his sacrifice to the altar, through "pleasure and pain." Like a night watchman fortuitously chasing one to his beloved, they have brought him to an unknown "palace gate," wonder of wonders, joy of joys, "in the evening at the end of my journey." Dharma blossoms from the fullness of the tree. Such was the course of Tagore's own dharma, as that of many poets, East and West.

In *Creative Unity* in 1922, Tagore sets down in the introduction the terms of discussion as his basic synthesis of values drawn from the Upanishads. He finds unity within his own person of the "immense mass of multitude to a single point," all united in himself, whether "mental, physical, chemical." "The One in me knows the universe of the many." Setting the focus of the whole book, he states, "This One in me is creative" and expresses itself through endless forms of poetry, painting, and music," "endless variety" of life. The One "seeks itself in others." "The One is infinite," "the One is Love":

To give perfect expression to the One, the Infinite, through the harmony of the many; to the One, the Love, through the sacrifice of self, is the object alike of our individual life and our society.

This passage might very well be the most succinct expression Tagore ever made about his entire conception of what he saw himself seeking to accomplish as a human being and a poet and what should be the goal of society.

In the first chapter of *Creative Unity*, "The Poet's Religion," Tagore probes the connection between his thinking and the English Romantic poets William Wordsworth, John Keats, Percy Bysshe Shelley, and others, speaking especially of Keats' "Ode to a Grecian Urn," finding that "truth reveals itself in beauty." True to his own youthful study of English literature, both in India and England, Tagore continues, "This is the poet's religion." Yet he excoriates,

> Those who are habituated to the rigid framework of sectarian creeds will find such a religion as this too indefinite and elastic. No doubt it is so, but only because its ambition is not to shackle the Infinite and tame it for domestic use; but rather to help our consciousness to emancipate itself from materialism. It is as indefinite as the morning, and yet as luminous; it calls our thoughts, feelings, and actions into freedom, and feeds them with light. In the poet's religion we find no doctrine or injunction, but rather the attitude of our entire being towards a truth which is ever to be revealed in its own endless creation.

It would be a misreading to think of Tagore as merely repeating the Romantics. It is the expression of the Infinite through beauty that he emphasizes, through all the forms of existence. It is not that poets create their own religion, as the orthodox might decry, but find and experience the Infinite in the Book of Creation, realizing the Infinite is not ultimately an organization or an exterior form, but significantly an "attitude" about life. Tagore himself feels how vague his "poet's religion" may sound and attempts to defend it against charges of "too indefinite and elastic." It could be argued that what he does is reminiscent of many Western poets, such as Emerson who chose to leave the Unitarian Church in 1832 "to make his own," shortly after

Rammohan Roy had extensively associated with Unitarians and had even published through their missionary press in Calcutta in the 1820s. East and West have had over a hundred years of such attempts, ending in failure and futility. Tagore's own reputation in India has suffered a decline and diminution over the last three decades or more for precisely the same reason, even in India, while those filled with misplaced nostalgia and longing misread him seeking to enlist him in their desire for a return to an Ayodhya that never existed. In most ways Tagore's sensibility was highly liberal and progressive. He wanted society to move forward, not backward. Such criticism is not uniquely applicable to Tagore but applies to modernity, East and West, for all have been drawn into its vortex. The traditional religions have long been in decline, and Tagore's idealism was but one instance among many, though a particularly brilliant and beautiful variety, an exquisite Eastern blossom growing towards fullness.

Answering those of ordinary mind, against the universal carnage of World War I, Tagore at the end of the chapter in *Creative Unity* writes,

Men of great faith have always called us to wake up to great expectations, and the prudent have always laughed at them and said that these did not belong to reality. But the poet in man knows that reality is a creation, and human reality has to be called forth from its obscure depth by man's faith which is creative. There was a day when the human reality was the brutal reality. That was the only capital we had with which to begin our career. But age after age there has come to us the call of faith, which said against all the evidence of fact: "You are more than you appear to be, more than your circumstances seem to warrant. You are to attain the impossible, you are immortal." The unbelievers had laughed and tried to kill the faith. But faith grew stronger with the strength of martyrdom and at her bidding higher realities have been created over the strata of the lower. Has not a new age come to-day, borne by thunder-clouds, ushered in by a universal agony of suffering? Are we not waiting to-day for a great call of faith, which will say to us: "Come out of your present limitations. You are to attain the impossible, you are immortal."

I would argue that, unlike "the poet's religion" or Romanticism, East or West, Tagore expresses here a very deep insight into the creation of personal and social unity and order. It doesn't just come out of thin air. It is a creation, not merely by poets, but by man, all of us, an act of faith against the "brutal reality" of our animal past and current situation, an affirmation of what is the deepest and most true in human nature, an "attitude" about what in fact makes us uniquely human, our consciousness, and its ineffable link with immortality and the infinite. Tagore sounds much of this clarion call again in 1941, against the second collapse of the world into brutal horror, in "The Crisis in Civilization," which I discuss further in my book *The Grove of the Eumenides: Essays on Literature, Criticism, and Culture*.

Rammohan Roy and Debendranath Tagore, the entire complicated movement from the Brahmo Sabha and Brahmo Samaj forward to Rabindranath was right to try to recover what was the most universal in the Upanishads and Sanskrit scriptures. The tempest of modernity, as in the West, with similar projects of recovery and renewal, resulted in a similar outcome, none of which gainsay the veracity of the underlying realities, which is why Tagore's appeal to a "new age come today" rings true to me, beyond even his own idealism, strikes a note that rises above the "brutal reality" of "wealth and power" to affirm "the call of faith," of immortality, "ushered in by a universal agony of suffering," again standing as he did just at the end of World War I. To this extent, I continue to believe Tagore forges forward into universality, not backwards into fantasy. For me, this is why Tagore is one of the most important global voices and examples, in literature and culture, along with Tolstoy, who worked on a highly parallel track seeking the universal, much more than Tagore perhaps ever understood, since Tolstoy's *Calendar of Wisdom*, a collection of excerpts drawing from all the great religions, never really found its way to an international readership and then was suppressed by the Soviets for decades until their demise.

After discussing the hermitages of the forest, the Upanishads, Vaishnava and Baul poetry, Rammohan Roy and Emperor Akbar, Tagore touches on what is for our time still the major problem and necessity confronting mankind:

> In the present age, with its facility of communication, geographical barriers have almost lost their reality, and the great federation of men, which is waiting either to find its true scope or to break asunder in a final catastrophe, is not a meeting of individuals, but of various human races. Now the problem before us is of one single country, which is this earth, where the races as individuals must find both their freedom of self-expression and their bond of federation. Mankind must realise a unity, wider in range, deeper in sentiment, stronger in power than ever before. Now that the problem is large, we have to solve it on a bigger scale, to realise the God in man by a larger faith and to build the temple of our faith on a sure and world-wide basis.

Tagore's insightful 1916 *Nationalism*, lectures in the United States and Japan, laid much of the foundation of his thinking regarding international federation. Not only had World War I recently ended with the destruction of much of Europe, revealing its spiritual and moral bankruptcy, but Woodrow Wilson, to whom Tagore had unsuccessfully tried to dedicate the book, had failed in his attempt to have the United States join the League of Nations after creating it through the Treaty of Versailles. There may also be an allusion in this passage to Alfred Tennyson's own reference in his poem "Locksley Hall" to "the Parliament of man, the Federation of the world." Nevertheless, Tagore is right that "the problem before us is of one single country, which is the earth." His call for mankind to achieve a higher unity than the nation state remains our quandary and our only hope subsequent to the even worse destruction of World War II, the Cold War, and the vastly devastating nuclear arsenal that is still endangering our planet. His almost instinctual call to "a bigger scale," essentially global, "to realise the God in man by a larger faith" represents a compelling appeal, both when he wrote it, and now, basically ninety years later. The destabilizing forces in our own time are so complex and volatile, from terrorism to the environment, evoking visions of degradation and collapse on a massive scale, that I believe the world must not only remember and honor such voices as Tagore's but actually follow them by truly working in a serious and concerted way to develop and expand the United Nations into a fully functioning, globally representative, democratic system that gives expression to the Will of the Peoples of Planet Earth beyond the lethal rivalries, worldwide economic crisis, international corporate greed, and extreme nationalism that now threatens our survival. Tagore demonstrates in this passage he was not a dreamy, out-of-touch poet wandering in the ancient forests of India but very much had his finger on the pulse of the modern patient and had prescribed the essential, salutary medicine. Before it is too late, we human beings must choose our God-given unity as a species and ban together for our common welfare, safety, and dignity.

In 1927 Tagore wrote a poem, here in his own translation from *Poems* (1942), that perfectly expresses much of his thinking in *Creative Unity*:

The world today is wild with the delirium of hatred,
the conflicts are cruel and unceasing in anguish,
crooked are its paths, tangled its bonds of greed.
All creatures are crying for a new birth of thine,
O Thou of boundless life,
save them, rouse thine eternal voice of hope,
let Love's lotus with its inexhaustible treasure of honey

open its petals in thy light.
O Serene, O Free,
in thine immeasurable mercy and goodness
wipe away all dark stains from the heart of this earth.

Thou giver of immortal gifts
give us the power of renunciation
and claim from us our pride.
In the splendor of a new sunrise of wisdom
let the blind gain their sight
and let life come to the souls that are dead.
O Serene, O Free,
in thine immeasurable mercy and goodness
wipe away all dark stains from the heart of this earth.

Man's heart is anguished with the fever of unrest, with the
poison of self-seeking,
with a thirst that knows no end.
Countries far and wide flaunt on their foreheads
the blood-red mark of hatred.
Touch them with thy right hand,
make them one in spirit,
bring harmony into their life,
bring rhythm of beauty.
O Serene, O Free,
in thinc immeasurable mercy and goodness
wipe away all dark stains from the heart of this earth.

After the apocalypse of World War I and the utter obstinacy
of the world community to learn anything from the experience,
whether in Europe, the United States of America, or the East, as
in China, Tagore accurately describes the world as "wild with
the delirium of hatred." Cruel conflicts follow one another,
exploitation of the masses, tangled in "bonds of greed." "All
creatures" seem to cry out for "a new birth," while the stanza
turns into a prayer, addressing "O thou of boundless life," "O

Serene, O Free," appealing for the cleansing and renovation of "the heart of this earth." The speaker places his hope in "a new sunrise of wisdom," the blind regaining "their sight." Man is wracked with "the poison of self-seeking," "countries far and wide" bear the marks of bloodlust. The poet-seer appeals to the Divine Being, on behalf of suffering humanity, to "make them one in spirit, bring harmony into their life," seeking a way forward to build, as it were, "the temple of our faith on a sure and world-wide basis."

In his book *The Religion of Man* in 1930, delivered as the Hibbert Lectures at Manchester College, Oxford, Tagore further meditates on the need of what he had called for in *Creative Unity*, "to realise the God in man in a larger faith." Trying perhaps to spell out its details, Tagore writes that "in this idea of unity" man "realizes the eternal in his life" and "consciousness of this unity is spiritual, and our effort to be true to it is our religion." Like the Bauls, Tagore has dispensed with all images, temples, and ceremonials, declaring in his songs "the divinity of man" expressing love for the Supreme Person. Tagore often quotes in his books, "*Advaitam* is *anandam*; the infinite One is Infinite Love." Expanding on the Upanishads, he explains, "The truth that is infinite dwells in the ideal of unity which we find in the deeper relatedness. This truth of realization is not in space, it can only be realized in one's own inner spirit," which is to say what all the great religions and religious teachers have said, that when one experiences the realization and presence of God, a dramatic change of consciousness and action takes place. Faith based on the exterior things of the earth falls short of the very nature of what's involved in worship of the Divine Presence.

Along with discussing in *The Religion of Man* Buddhism, Zoroastrianism, the Bhagavad Gita, and Taoism, Tagore gives the reader his own beautiful translation of the Gayatri:

Let me contemplate the adorable splendour of Him who created the earth, the air and the starry spheres, and sends the power of comprehension within our minds.

Analogous to the Jewish and Christian *Shema*, in its importance to the religious tradition of the Upanishads, Tagore writes that the Gayatri "produced a sense of serene exaltation in me," which he daily meditated on, uniting "in one stream of creation my mind and the outer world." He continues by conceding that "It is evident that my religion is a poet's religion, and neither that of an orthodox man of piety nor that of a theologian," that it "comes to me through the same unseen and trackless channel as does the inspiration of my songs. Somehow they were wedded to each other." As with the Romantics, there is a mysterious source for Tagore's sense of transcendence, though more grounded in what can appear to Westerners as fairly orthodox texts and traditions, yet the Bauls were not part of mainstream Brahmanism whatsoever, nor was the entire history of his family's involvement with the Brahmo Samaj and what it represented. All of this provided Tagore with a rich experience and personal tradition of spiritual seeking beyond the confines of the more orthodox pathways of conventional Hinduism.

Tagore relates in *The Religion of Man* how all these strands in his biography and background culminated in his mystical experience, mentioned earlier, on Sudder Street, and his poem of 1883, "The Awakening." Similarly, I found myself compelled to write my poem "Dawn of a New Day," in my chapbook *Crow Hunting*, in an attempt to understand and express the nature of the experience. Tagore recounts how "I felt that I had found my religion at last, the religion of Man, in which the infinite became defined in humanity and came close to me so as to need my love and cooperation." The same ardor often found expression in his recurring theme of "Jivan Devata, the Lord of my life":

Thou who art the innermost Spirit of my being, art thou pleased,
Lord of my life? For I gave to thee my cup filled with all the pain and delight that the crushed grapes of my heart had surrendered, I wove with the rhythm of colours and songs the cover for thy bed,

and with the molten gold of my desires I fashioned playthings
for thy passing hours.
I know not why thou chosest me for thy partner,

Lord of my life!

Didst thou store my days and nights, my deeds and dreams for
the alchemy of thy art, and string in the chain of thy music my
songs of autumn

and spring, and gather the flowers from my mature moments for
thy crown?
I see thine eyes gazing at the dark of my heart,

Lord of my life,

I wonder if my failures and wrongs are forgiven. For many were
my days without service and nights of forgetfulness; futile were
the flowers that faded in the shade not
offered to thee.

Often the tired strings of my lute slackened at the strain of thy
tunes. And often at the ruin of wasted hours my desolate
evenings were filled with tears.
But have my days come to their end at last,

Lord of my life,

while my arms round thee grow limp, my kisses losing their
truth? Then break up the meeting of this languid day. Renew
the old in me in fresh forms of delight; and let the wedding
come once again in a new ceremony of life.

Tagore is the W. B. Yeats of India, the Irish poet he didn't really
know much about after receiving the Nobel Prize. In 1912,
when he had met Yeats in London, the latter was still absorbed

with Irish Celtic myth, his *A Vision* and the poems it made possible lay years ahead of him. Equally opaque to Yeats was Tagore's own long journey on his way to London. They were each in the hands of their inner spirit more than either knew about the other. Also, as one scholar has said, neither Yeats's introduction to the *Gitanjali*, nor Tagore's 1912 essay on Yeats, goes much beyond generalities. Tagore's myth had already become as multifarious as what Yeats would eventually achieve. The Lord of Life was in control of the poets' religion, all the clearer in retrospect. Krishna Kripalani, who truly merits the title of scholar, approaches this understanding when he observes,

> Though by birth a Brahmin and the son of a great Hindu reformer, Tagore's feeling for Hinduism was strictly eclectic and was more or less confined to his admiration of the philosophic wisdom of the Upanishads and the literary heritage of Sanskrit. For Brahminism as such, for its priestly authority and the tyranny of its regimented social organization, he had nothing but contempt (175-76).

"Jivan Devata," a theme on which Tagore wrote many variations, evokes his "poet's religion," "strictly eclectic," drawing loyally from the Upanishads and the broad mystic traditions that he found capable of sustaining his universal vision of spirituality. He found it preferable to the rigid convolutions of Brahminism and more conducive to a productive social order for India in the modern world, though it should be remembered, late in life, in an introduction to a collection of scriptures, Tagore acknowledged about the Upanishads that "their emphasis was too intellectual, and did not sufficiently explore the approach to Reality through love and devotion [bhakti] (Krishna Dutta 30). His addresses on education, agriculture, and Indian history in the 1920s and '30s demonstrate that while his literary muse could fly with the intoxicated mystics and Jivan Devata, yet his feet were firmly planted, down to earth, in the good rich soil of India, more so at times than Gandhi's bare feet.

Tagore's poetry is not all petitioning Jivan Devata. He does understand the pressure and arguments of modernity, observing in *The Religion of Man* that

> We find in modern literature that something like a chuckle of an exultant disillusionment is becoming contagious, and the knights-errant of the cult of arson are abroad, setting fire to our time-honoured altars of worship, proclaiming that the images enshrined on them, even if beautiful, are made of mud. They say that it has been found out that the appearances in human idealism are deceptive, that the underlying mud is real. From such a point of view, the whole of creation may be said to be a gigantic deception, and the billions of revolving electric specks that have the appearance of "you" or "me" should be condemned as bearers of false evidence.

It's not that Tagore ignores modernity and just blithely sails off into mysticism out of mindless nostalgia. He understands the reasons for disillusionment and is himself disillusioned with Western civilization and its failure to live up to its highest claims, as articulated in Christianity, and which, as we've seen, he repeatedly stated after World War I. It's that Tagore believes the surest response is "the inborn criterion of the real," "the rose must be more satisfactory than its constituent gases," existing truly in a "perfect harmony" of its parts. He emphasizes "wholeness" over the clever ability to deconstruct. "The animal in the savage has been transferred into higher stages in the civilized man" by "a magical grouping" of the unruly and disillusioning materials of the human being, "curbing and stressing in proper places," creating "a unique value to our personality in all its completeness." This is Tagore's answer to the nihilism of modernity: "To keep alive our faith in the reality of the ideal perfection is the function of civilization." Rather than surrendering to the "realism" of modern literature, Tagore argues it contains a limited portion of human experience and truth. At their best, poetry, literature, and all the arts affirm the fullness of the human being, strengthening the foundation of civilization at the deepest level.

As with his thought on the rose, many of his writings reflect on the nature of science and its relation to religion and poetry. His thinking is often refreshing since it comes from a cultural viewpoint other than Christian and Western, both of which have done so much to muddy the waters during recent centuries. For instance, in *Sadhana* (1913) he writes, already arguing against a secular, dehumanizing science, what I would call Scientism, that the world is more than rocks and water and "the play of forces." The man of "spiritual vision" sees deeper into creation, appreciating the wholeness of "natural phenomenon," that the One manifests "its living presence" in nature and in the human being. Tagore's spirituality is often akin to that of more primordial religions, such as American Indians, that God imbues nature with transcendence and oneness. "Science collects facts" and statistics, creating "mental pictures" which are not stable and are in fact "evanescent." The picture of the struggle for existence leaves out reciprocity, love for others, and the sacrifice of self, inspired by love, "the positive element in life," none of which gainsays the laws of science, for the laws are "not something apart from us." They are "our own." Tagore argues again that the "universal law is one with our own power." Through science "we come to know more of the laws of nature" and "tend to attain a universal body," "worldwide." Science expands "our physical strength" and abilities through locomotion, steam, electricity, and other forces. In an incredible statement, especially for 1913, he says, "there is no limit to our powers, for we are not outside the universal power which is the expression of universal law." Many of the maladies and limitations of human existence "are not absolute."

Returning to the flower analogy, Tagore details its many constituent parts and biological functions in leading to the fruit of a plant. Science argues a flower has no relation to "the heart of men," nor is the notion that it is the emblem of something else anything but imaginary. "Beauty," responds Tagore, "becomes its only qualification." Why do modern human beings choose to believe in a flower's practical nature and yet reject its human influence? The outer truth but not the inner? In *Sadhana*, the Upanishads provide his text: "Verily from the everlasting joy do all objects have their birth." There is a natural function and a spiritual one, the latter "like a messenger from the King," "from our great lover," "a message from the other shore":

> Through our progress in science the wholeness of the world and our oneness with it is becoming clearer to our mind. When this perception of the perfection of unity is not merely intellectual, when it opens out our whole being into a luminous consciousness of the all, then it becomes a radiant joy, an overspreading love. Our spirit finds its larger self in the whole world, and is filled with an absolute certainty that it is immortal. It dies a hundred times in its enclosures of self; for separateness is doomed to die, it cannot be made eternal. But it never can die where it is one with the all, for there is its truth, its joy.

In *Personality*, another set of lectures delivered in the United States in 1916, several times at Unitarian Churches, Tagore further explains, "A flower is nothing when we analyse it, but it is positively a flower when we enjoy it." Again, his point highlights the wholeness of our personal experience of a flower and the joy it gives. I believe Tagore's emphasis on unity and the role of science in expanding man's awe before its discoveries and results are all the more insightful as we have progressed further along in our scientific advancement in understanding creation and the cosmos. Yet Tagore rightly criticized the West for being mainly concerned with the extension "outwards," to the neglect of "inner consciousness which is the field of fulfillment." His interest and dialogue with science runs throughout his books, unexpectedly resulting in a textbook, in 1937, *Our Universe*, surveying scientific knowledge from the world of atoms to the world of stars, asking Jivan Devata, before "the plants, stars and the sun, / Are you not as real as they are?"

I cannot write about Tagore without reflecting on his visit to the Soviet Union in 1930. Tagore has often been criticized for a failure to appreciate the extent to which he was deceived and duped by Mussolini and then by the communist state. I have often shared that opinion and still do, but now think that it is fair to say in Tagore's defense that such criticism also reflects a Cold War mentality that neglects to understand Tagore's reasons for making the trip to the USSR, related to bettering education and agriculture in India, and fails to listen to the words he carefully chooses while a guest in a foreign land. Tagore is much more critical of the "grievous mistakes" than he is often given credit for. His last interview with a reporter of the state newspaper *Izvestia* in Moscow reveals clearly how aware Tagore was of, as he diplomatically phrased it, "certain contradictions to the great mission which you have undertaken." He was so candid that the interview was never published in *Izvestia* until after the collapse of the Soviet Union in the late 1980s, though it did appear at the time in England:

Are you doing your ideas a service by arousing in the minds of those under your training, anger, class hatred and revengefulness against those not sharing your ideal, against those whom you consider to be your enemies? ...does not humanity include those who do not agree with your aim? Just as you try to help the peasants who have other ideas than yours about religion, economics, and social life... should you not have the same mission to those other people who have other ideals than your own? ...There must be disagreement where minds are allowed to be free. If you have a mission which includes all humanity, you must, for the sake of that living humanity, acknowledge the existence of differences of opinion. ...Violence begets violence and blind stupidity. Freedom of mind is needed for the reception of truth; terror hopelessly kills it. ...for the sake of humanity I hope that you may never create a vicious force of violence which will go on weaving an interminable chain of violence and cruelty. Already you have inherited much of this legacy from the Tsarist regime. It is the worst legacy you possibly could have. ...Why not try to destroy this one also?

It is an interview that perhaps some people in India today who in desperation feel Marxism offers hope might kindly be encouraged to read and seriously reflect on. Too many Asian nations have already fallen into the abyss and gulag of Marxism, with uniformly traumatic and tragic results. How terrible for India if it were ever to happen to her, ignoring the voice of its greatest poet-seer. Nevertheless, given his description of the USSR in "The Crisis in Civilization," it is a valid question to what extent Tagore influenced events in West Bengal and elsewhere, unwittingly contributed to unfortunate developments.

It is difficult sometimes for people to understand why the West does not respond more to Tagore. He can, like Gandhi, be considered almost an infallible god. Some think of him as universal, as, in a sense, I indeed do, one of the most universal poets of the 20th Century. No poet in the West can compare with Tagore. American poets have come to pride themselves on how small they actually are, vying with one another for the dubious honor. The truth is that for Westerners, even some Asians, Tagore is not universal enough. For we need a whole new vision of what it means to be human, a new vision of life, its spiritual, which is to say, human, humane nature, *jen* in the Chinese meaning. Yet it is still possible, despite how bleak and nihilistic the local and international scene may appear, for we live in a time of spiritual decline when even a church with the history of the Unitarian Universalists can announce, at least in the higher echelons, that it has moved away from all forms of transcendence, though with much diversity at the local and individual levels. It is certainly the best poets and writers, artists in all forms, like Tagore, who have the spiritual sensitivity to sense and detect and articulate the vision needed. Not politics, but *vision*. For man is his thought, as the Upanishads rightly understood and taught, as did Tagore. When our understanding of life becomes decadent, it is precisely the spiritual Imagination, the most characteristically human capacity distinguishing us from the animals that can aid us in our plight, now global, for ourselves and our children, our children's children's children, all succeeding generations of this spinning Planet Earth. I have carefully traced and suggested how far more universal Tagore is than many poets in the West, well into the 20th Century, but ultimately that we all live still in a world when universality lies beyond, as it did for Tagore. Marking a tremendous stride in the right direction, Tagore has encouraged the world to follow him, remembering and honoring our spiritual heritage, beyond materialism, so blatantly bankrupt now all around the globe, toward the Divine Unity we so dearly need to recover, trusting the Transcendent One to guide us, as only He can, working through the lives of men and women, including His gift of science, into that Promised Time of peace and joy.

Tagore and Literary Adaptation

Accidentally including three or four poems by another poet among his collection of short poems, *Fireflies* (Lekhan), what Tagore did was discussed in April of 2002, in a different context, by Richard Posner's "On Plagiarism," in *The Atlantic Monthly*:

> The writer who plagiarizes out of... forgetfulness, the latter being the standard defense when one is confronted with proof of one's plagiarism.

It was a mistake. Tagore immediately owned it. He was human, too, and graciously admitted he had erred, when it was pointed out to him, dealing with many manuscripts from years ago, jumbled together. Why should it be held against him by later sticklers?

Unlike his honest mistake, using material from another writer in a different context for literary purposes should not be confused with the niceties of English 101 pedagogy. There are other kinds of borrowing and using material from other writers, of which much of English literature would be the worse without:

> Shakespeare himself was a formidable plagiarist in the broad sense in which I'm using the word. The famous description in *Antony and Cleopatra* of Cleopatra on her royal barge is taken almost verbatim from a translation of Plutarch's life of Mark Antony: "on either side of her, pretty, fair boys apparelled as painters do set forth the god Cupid, with little fans in their hands, with which they fanned wind upon her" becomes "on each side her / Stood pretty dimpled boys, like smiling Cupids, / With divers-colour'd fans, whose wind did seem / To glow the delicate cheeks which they did cool." (Notice how Shakespeare improved upon the original.)

There are many instances of such "plagiarism" in Shakespeare, one of the most moving in *The Tempest* from Ovid, in which Prospero abjures his art. Similarly, according to Jorge Luis Borges, in his second lecture on English literature, the poet of Beowulf quotes Virgil and interpolates other lines into the poem, "interspersed in the text." Posner continues,

> In *The Waste Land*, T. S. Eliot "stole" the famous opening of Shakespeare's barge passage, "The barge she sat in, like a burnish'd throne, / Burn'd on the water" becoming "The Chair she sat in, like a burnished throne, / Glowed on the marble.
>
> If these are examples of plagiarism, then we want more plagiarism. They show that not all unacknowledged copying is "plagiarism" in the pejorative sense. Although there is no formal acknowledgment of copying in my examples, neither is there any likelihood of deception. And the copier has added value to the original—this is not slavish copying…. Eliot and Mann wanted their audience to recognize their borrowings.

I would argue, the more expansive the scope, the more necessary to his craft—that the poet will find himself compelled to lean on the tradition to reach his audience, educate it, realizing readers cannot be assumed to follow the sweep and depth of his own study, unless he pays tribute to the original sources within his work, adapting and raising the material to the service of his vision. What is germane, is, as Posner suggests, does it work? Does the poet lift the sources to something *new*? Tagore's little gaffe never reached the level of these questions that no conscientious poet can fail to ask him or herself because it truly was a mistake.

It seems to me that Posner is right, though, about Shakespeare, T. S. Eliot, and Thomas Mann. They stole whatever they needed and wanted, leaving it to readers to recognize the sources, as extended allusion, if nothing else, in some cases. Footnotes in a creative work would be contradictory by nature and disruptive of the reader's concentration. The proverbial pedant might think highly of them, especially today, struggling to get tenure, what better way to justify one's self than alleging plagiarism and creating an uproar, preening self-righteously, but should tremble before Shakespeare's lampooning Polonius. The Bard knew what that kind of thing was worth.

For a writer it's hard to know sometimes what to do. I've read widely for forty years, yet can't assume the reader in the US or elsewhere has, quite the reverse, in an age of nauseating, dehumanizing specialization. How do I attempt to embody and represent the fullness of human reflection without "using" the originals? I went through much agonizing over all this through the years, but decided the tale must come first. Its roots must be allowed to draw from the soil of literature and culture whatever they need to produce and sustain their fruit. Many writers have done that. I studied extensively many years ago the original Puritan documents that both Hawthorne and the playwright Arthur Miller used, put to similar uses. Ultimately, there's no easy answer, I suppose, but hope that there will be those who will acknowledge I serve the higher aims of my vision.

Much of the literary world has become closed off in doctrinaire nihilism and rhetoric, cocooned in the Myth of the Enlightenment, clutching to its chest its Goddess of Reason, ignoring the extent to which these ideas have led to or participated in many of the most bloody upheavals of modernity, around the globe, and lie at the core of many of our continuing dilemmas. Intellectual rigidity, politicization, and closed-mindedness supplant the search for truth. In this sense, there's little difference between the "truth" of the complacent cultural elite and various fundamentalists that they castigate. Most cultural organs and publications are fanatically devoted to the secular god of modernity. Like the worst of Christian fundamentalists that many enjoy caricaturing, lumping all people of spiritual sensibility together with them, liberals and progressives, in and out of the university, can be just as closed off to other visions of life and human possibility.

Basically noting this, the theoretical physicist Peter Higgs, of the Higgs boson particle, has observed in *The Guardian* (December 26, 2012) about Richard Dawkins that

> What Dawkins does too often is to concentrate his attack on fundamentalists. But there are many believers who are just not fundamentalists.... Fundamentalism is another problem. I mean, Dawkins in a way is almost a fundamentalist himself, of another kind.

Especially in the light of Quantum Physics, I think these are also refreshing and interesting passages from Peter Higgs:

> The growth of our understanding of the world through science weakens some of the motivation which makes people believers. But that's not the same thing as saying they're incompatible. It's just that I think some of the traditional reasons for belief, going back thousands of years, are rather undermined.

> But that doesn't end the whole thing. Anybody who is a convinced but not a dogmatic believer can continue to hold his belief. It means I think you have to be rather more careful about the whole debate between science and religion than some people have been in the past.

I have had the books of Richard Dawkins, Daniel Dennett, Sam Harris, and Christopher Hitchens for a long time, and have read chunks of them, on and off, following their arguments in various ways for many years. A year ago I read, with a group of Unitarian Universalists, Greg Epstein's *Good Without God*, sort of an attempt to turn atheism into a religion. There have been and are other such attempts. To my mind, they are logical descendants of modernism and Scientism, and I don't find that persuasive, especially when they become as fanatical and smugly self-righteous as any fundamentalist Christian or whatever. Peter Higgs is a more balanced and nuanced voice.

What constitutes "religion" or *a* religion, is much of the question to me. I wouldn't include organizations and institutionalized "religions." By the time that happens, it seems to me that religion is no longer the concern. Cultural politics is often no more a search for truth than fundamentalist sects. I try to grapple with all this in my epic poem. I think the language of poetry, both a particle and a wave, a form of epistemology, is the best way in which to do that.

The media of poorly educated journalists, too, often uses a definition of "religion" that is a caricature to my mind, very narrow and tiresome, the "old man with a long beard." The cheap journalistic strawman. Awe before the mystery and majesty of creation is beyond all that, experience of that, not abstractions. Exclusive claims to truth demonstrate a certain problem in their own way, whether "religion," literary "theory," or science. The modern understanding of religion and spirituality is much of our problem today, as the exclusivisms of all the traditional religions have shown themselves ever further out of touch with experience, life as it has come to be lived, which is much more global and human, universal, than the narrow, isolated cultures of the past in which they all arose. The eyes of the child, or poet, before nature, the awesomeness of the cosmos, as it continues to unfold deeper and deeper *out there*, is the quintessential response to life and is part of what I try to explore in my epic.

For years now with Facebook opening up access for global communication, I have wondered and hoped that perhaps India in some way holds the key for confronting modern nihilism and turning the tide, East and West, if you will, to allude to Matthew Arnold's "Dover Beach." I am not one who naively thinks India is the "mystic East." My essay about India and Indian literature makes precisely that point, "India's Kali Yuga," about the loss of a spiritual vision in various modern Indian writers, as in the West.

T. S. Eliot, in his essay on Philip Massinger, in *The Sacred Wood*, speaks to borrowing from other authors and "cultural appropriation," as it were, which my marginalia tells me I read decades ago:

> One of the surest of tests is the way in which a poet borrows. Immature poets imitate; mature poets steal; bad poets deface what they take, and good poets make it into something better, or at least something different. The good poet welds his theft into a whole of feeling which is unique, utterly different from that from which it was torn; the bad poet throws it into something which has no cohesion. A good poet will usually borrow from authors remote in time, or alien in language, or diverse in interest. Chapman borrowed from Seneca; Shakespeare and Webster from Montaigne... (Methuen & Co edition, 1972 reprint. 125.)

I read this choice passage from *The Sacred Wood* in my twenties, but had largely lost all memory of it, absorbing it really, for it seems the idea has always been with me. As an aside, the "sacred wood" refers to Sir James Frazer's *The Golden Bough* and the wood and grove of Greek and Western early religious experience. It's partly why I named my collection of essays *The Grove of the Eumenides*, although thinking primarily of Sophocles' grove in *Oedipus at Colonus*.

Eliot's passage fits precisely how the old masters can be given a new lease on life. Again, that was very much in my mind in writing my epic poem. In the US, it can be a common criticism that many young would-be poets no longer read the work of important writers of only a few decades ago, let alone the ancients, East and West. Everything has become one's personal life, some dehumanizing academic theory or formalism, obsession with language and technique, the usual trivialities of

71

decadent literary periods. Despite all that, I hope I have honored the great masters, who have meant so much to me throughout my life, who still speak to our time, if we will but listen carefully, with reverence.

Saul Bellow's *Ravelstein*
The Closing of the American Soul
2009

When Saul Bellow's novel *Ravelstein* was published in 2000, I did not rush out and buy a copy but closely followed the many reviews that began to appear. I had read almost all of Bellow's work up to his last novel but felt for some reason that the time was not right to read *Ravelstein*, despite my having ravenously devoured Allan Bloom's *The Closing of the American Mind* when it had been published in 1987, and anything related to it. I trusted my intuition and attended to other interests, while more reviews continued to come out. Occasionally, I would stumble on one and read it, thinking *Ravelstein* was a book that I'd have to read someday. Then in 2005 I bought a copy when I happened upon it in a bookstore, but I didn't read it. I put it on a shelf, waiting for the right moment. This fall, a year and a half into working on writing my epic poem, I realized I needed Saul Bellow's help. I needed to know how things really stood with the Jews. Even more than *Commentary Magazine*, I knew I could count on Saul Bellow to tell me the truth. He never lied to me in the past. I remembered *Ravelstein* and retrieved it. The right moment in the life of my soul had come.

After reading *Ravelstein*, I reread most of the articles and reviews I had been collecting for years. I was struck by the shoddiness of the typical piece of writing published in national newspapers, magazines, and academic journals. Schools of journalism might provide their students with a modicum of technical training but certainly are not capable of cultivating the necessary sensibility to read and understand a subtle and complex literary creation, while English departments, under the *rigor mortis* of Deconstruction and the like, have abandoned and betrayed literature and poetry, rendering many of their students incapable of even writing a clear, intelligible sentence. The review that interested me was by a writer, Cynthia Ozick, who insightfully perceives what Saul Bellow is about, though she only touches on Bellow's ruminations on the soul in passing, in *The New Republic*, "'Soul' being his most polemical term." These curious facts fascinate me and convey something very important about the present state of cultural affairs. We have lost the soul and few can even recognize it. Few are willing to discuss it.

Many of the thirty or more reviews focus on the surface layers of *Ravelstein*, emphasizing it's a *roman-a-clef*; that is, the characters correspond to real people, Allan Bloom, as Abe Ravelstein, and Chick, as Saul Bellow himself. But the novel is much more than that, much more than mere biography. Ozick is very perceptive about that fact, unlike the journalistic hacks so much of the media presents as "reviewers." Much is sensationally made of Bellow's disclosing Bloom's homosexuality and death from AIDS, as though that really amounted to everything in terms of the book. Technical critiques, plot summaries, gossip, and so on, all substitute for understanding and interpretation. Bellow tells us what the book is about if only we'll listen, remain open and sensitive to detail.

Abe Ravelstein, a university professor of political philosophy, though Chick at times dismisses him as such, achieves the rarest kind of success, a best selling book that turns him into a millionaire, Allan Bloom's own intellectually demanding book, *The Closing of the American Mind: How Higher Education Has Failed Democracy, and Impoverished the Souls of Today's Students* (1987):

> He had gone over the heads of the profs and the learned societies to speak directly to the great public. There are, after all, millions of people waiting for a sign. Many of them are university graduates (48).

Only "The great public" is worthy of a writer's aspiration. We live in a time when most writers are content to settle for a low, narrow, constrained, academic audience, a coterie, made up solely of people in university circles, "creative" writing programs, and so on, preaching to the choir. Allan Bloom and Bellow chose humanity, in all its plenitude, as much as could listen and understand, at a high and demanding level, as had Rabelais, Cervantes, and Shakespeare. The university does not captain the great ship of literature. Poets, playwrights, and novelists are the trustees of the literary tradition, not academicians. They are the last people poets should be writing for. The secondary crowd of secondary scholars write secondary things and achieve only secondary results. During the last eighty years, since the New Criticism, the Age of Criticism has only continued to devolve into ever more effete and alienated theories of life and literature, which have nearly sunk the great ship. American English departments have proven themselves unworthy stewards of the literary tradition, of what is noble in human nature, in the great public. When Polonius is left to run the culture, he destroys it with his dehumanizing abstractions.

In the novel, Ravelstein admits that Chick had suggested the idea of writing the book, believing Ravelstein only had to write up all his lecture notes to achieve a popular success. The interplay of their two characters shapes and structures the entire book, with Bellow often provocatively emphasizing the contrasts. Once Ravelstein dies, the novel continues because it is about the ideas of Bloom, their critique, and not the mere memoir Ravelstein had wanted. For in the end, it's the differences between Ravelstein and Chick that count in the overall meaning of the book and in the meaning of the resolution about life and death. Another significant theme is their reflections on the "viciousness" of modern history, as demonstrated by the Nazi treatment of the Jews and other East European atrocities. Ravelstein helps Chick to come to understand the dark side of history and humanity—"viciousness was universal."

Yet Chick informs the reader at one point that he is not writing about Ravelstein's ideas on the political philosophy of Western civilization since Plato, though Ravelstein thought he was essentially commissioning Chick to write a memoir of his life, believing Chick has the literary gift for it. The fact is, however, that Bellow does write about Allan Bloom's ideas, indeed, critiques them, as well as Bloom's life. In his treatment of Ravelstein, Bellow goes right to the core of Bloom's shortcomings, both as a thinker and as a man, which is not to say that Bellow doesn't give Ravelstein credit for his contribution to "the correct ordering of the soul." The original title of Ravelstein's book, Chick explains, was "Souls Without Longing," the Platonic longing for fullness of being, as in Plato's *Symposium* and Aristophanes, "the missing portion to complete" our highest, true self.

Repeatedly Chick discloses that Ravelstein is an atheist, a secular, assimilated Jew, hates his own father and family, fails to love his neighbors, is dying of AIDS, and other unfavorable, contradictory elements of his character and life. In recruiting Chick, Ravelstein had told him, "I want you to show me as you see me, without softness or sweeteners." If those were Allan Bloom's actual words, he was a brave man to invite America's greatest modern novelist to show him warts and all and definitely got what he asked for. Chick, interested in the "chicks," the real passions of life, more so than abstract ideas, now with his second wife, is advised by her, Rosamund, that Chick should "leave it to others to comment on his ideas," meaning Ravelstein's ideas. He responds, "Oh, I intend to. I'm going to leave intellectual matters to the experts," which resonates with a deceptive irony that ought to tip off any sensitive reader. Saul Bellow often had little respect for academic "experts." I've already mentioned he dismisses Ravelstein at times as a mere professor, a teacher.

Bellow is actually writing about the soul and the afterlife and chastens the failure of Allan Bloom to give them both their proper due. In one discussion of Platonic longing, Chick mockingly states, "Ravelstein was in real earnest about this quest driven by longing." Ravelstein looked for longing in his students, acquaintances, and friends. Chick describes himself as a Jew, though engaged and struggling with modernity, with religious conceptions implicitly within the more customary framework of Judaism. On the other hand, Ravelstein, the learned professor, is out on the edge, in every way, with "his esoteric system," almost counter-culture, like the students he criticizes in his book. By critiquing the life of Ravelstein, Bellow is critiquing the ideas of Allan Bloom, at a very deep level, for Bloom's book ultimately reflects its author's secular and atheistic outlook, even while it appears to affirm the transcendent values of Plato and the Greeks. Chick rams this home when he says, "for most of mankind the longings have, one way or another, been eliminated." Ultimately, this is just as true of the picture Chick paints of Ravelstein, "portrays," he self-deprecatingly puts it, and is Bellow's deepest criticism of him.

Near the end of the book in Chick's reflections on the afterlife, Chick reveals that even the brilliant atheist Abe Ravelstein, when confronted with the impending seriousness of death, accepted that there must be an afterlife. By then, Ravelstein had moved on from Greece and Athens to Jerusalem. Chick recounts earlier in the novel his memories as a child being intensely struck by the vivid experience, the "first epistemological impressions," of the sheer miracle of life, "the pictures," as he phrases it, of existence, his "intimate metaphysics." When Ravelstein, facing death from AIDS, asks Chick what he imagines death would be like, Chick answers it would mean the pictures would stop, which Ravelstein respectfully broods on. Chick reflects,

No one can give up on the pictures—the pictures might, yes they might continue. I wonder if anyone believes that the grave is all there is. No one can give up on the pictures. The pictures must and will continue. If Ravelstein the atheist-materialist had implicitly told me that he would see me sooner or later, he meant that he did not accept the grave to be the end. Nobody can and nobody does accept this. We just talk tough (222).

Striking at the heart of Allan Bloom's ideas, Saul Bellow reveals their weakest point, standing no more on a sure foundation, for all of Bloom's formidable intellectual accomplishment, than all the modern nihilists Bloom denounces. For Chick had earlier revealed, while discussing the pictures at length, that he, unlike Ravelstein, "had no intention, however, of removing, by critical surgery, the metaphysical lenses I was born with." Socratic "longing" is not enough and cannot alone restore the soul, neither for the individual nor the modern world, yet the scale of values made possible for Bloom a historical position from which he could critique modernity, but proved untenable when confronted with the grave.

In 2002 in an interview with Antonio Monda, published in *Do You Believe* (2007), available online on *The Jewish Daily Forward*, Bellow laconically answers the point-blank question "Do you believe in God?" with one word: "Yes." He dismisses further discussion, believing "it's a subject whose importance is diminished by conversation." A few years earlier, in 1999, Norman Manea interviewed Bellow, published eventually in 2007 in *Salmagundi*. The long, wide-ranging interview covers Bellow's life and personal views on many subjects. In it Bellow states,

> I stopped arguing with myself about belief in God. It's not a real question. The real question is how have I really felt all these years, and all these years I have believed in God; so there it is. What are you going to do about it? So it's not a question really of the intellect freeing itself from bondage, it's the question, first of all, of trying to decide whether this is bondage and then just accepting what you believe because that's all you can do by now (161).

Like Chick, and in the end even Ravelstein, Bellow didn't believe "the pictures stop." As with all of Saul Bellow's books, his probings at the soul of modernity is at the core of *Ravelstein*, and at the core of Chick's criticism of Bloom's ideas, of the groundless, unsustainable ideas of modernity. And so even Bellow near the end of his life could honestly acknowledge to Norman Manea that his earnestness "was more an experience of nostalgia for me than it was a spiritual reality." Yet the cloying political correctness of our secular, nihilistic age and the journalists, academicians, and writers so caught up in rigid adherence and obeisance to the ruling orthodoxy of Scientism, do not know what to make of a serious writer like Bellow who has the temerity actually to believe in and write about God, and such spiritual matters as the afterlife. Many choose to ignore this part of his work. This is the state of the human soul that is still with us, even as it has demonstrated so fully its bankruptcy as a vision of life in every department of human endeavor. Beyond the stale ideas of modernity, Bellow's down-to-earth answer to the ideas of Allan Bloom, as in the interview with Manea, quietly affirms, "all these years I have believed in God; so there it is."

Robert Hayden Under a High Window of Angell Hall[2]

It is hard for a man to find one kindred spirit among thousands of his fellows, and if at last, softened by our prayers, fate grants one, there comes the unexpected day, the unlooked for hour, which snatches him away, leaving an eternal emptiness. —John Milton, *Elegy for Damon* (tr Anna Beer)

As a young poet I had chosen not to go off to the university after high school, but followed what I thought of as the solitary examples of Robert Frost, E. A. Robinson, and other writers. For a few years, living and writing on an old broken-down farm in Oakland Township, Michigan, I tried on the singing robes of Emerson, Whitman, and others, eventually moving to Detroit, near Seven Mile and John R, having been born, at Deaconess Hospital on East Jefferson Avenue, where more than one line in my family tree has roots extending into the neighborhoods nearby, some back into the 19th Century. One day at the Detroit Public Library, I noticed a placard that a librarian had posted about the poet Robert Hayden. I sought out his books and read and immersed myself in his poetry, in time, deciding I would transfer to the University of Michigan in hope of studying with him. My dream came true more than I had ever expected, taking three classes with him, one in Recent Poetry, an independent study of Emily Dickinson, and a private tutorial in writing.

---

[2]A shorter version by half of this essay was presented at the Robert Hayden Conference and Poetry Tribute, The University of Michigan, Rackham Amphitheatre, November 1, 2013, and an excerpt from the canto "The Flight to the Moon," in which Hayden is a character. Youtu.be/A3P1kZOrUnQ

As I explain in my essay on Hayden in my book *The Grove of the Eumenides*, during the poetry class, he was diagnosed with cancer and was devastated by the prognosis. Looking back I think my writing for him essays on Countee Cullen and Pablo Neruda brought me to his attention, or an office visit, chance comments on literature, before long in and out of class. His own poetry had already worked its way deep into my consciousness. He knew I held him in high esteem and I felt it a duty to let him know it. In time he became not only older poet, master, mentor, but, I believe, mutually heart-felt friend, father, taking me increasingly into his confidence, hiring me as a secretary to help him get his papers somewhat in order, and allowing me entry into the private life of his home and family, often two or three afternoons a week for the last several months of his life. Robert Hayden is not merely a literary, academic subject to me but the pivotal personal relationship of my entire adult life.

I found in Hayden's writing a confrontation and engagement with injustice and modernity unlike anything else on the landscape of Post-World War II poetry. As a Detroiter myself, having been born in the City, with many childhood memories, eventually growing up in the suburbs, I was fascinated by Hayden's ability to evoke and probe the complex human experience of modern life, whether writing about Detroit and America's seemingly endless traumas with race, the wider sweep around the globe, or the spiritual profundities he intimated. Even more than Robert Lowell, Hayden's poetry always spoke to me at a deeper level of consciousness than any other post-war American poet.

Having written extensively elsewhere on Hayden in terms of race and poetry, I want to convey that early on I felt drawn to his grappling with the evils and violence that human beings perpetrate on one another. In "Words in the Mourning Time," evoking Vietnam, poem "III" offers a striking example:

He comes to my table in his hungry wounds
and his hunger. The flamed-out eyes,

their sockets dripping. The nightmare mouth.

He snatches food from my plate, raw
fingers bleeding, seizes my glass
and drinks, leaving flesh-fragments on its rim.

Horror incarnate. Vietnamese, napalmed. The horrifying
dehumanization of the image evokes and condemns what we
Americans have become, merciless in our military might,
imposing our will on others, our political and
military-industrial-congressional machine destroying anything
and anyone that stands in our way, carpet bombing nations into
submission, ignoring, in the case of Vietnam, the UN Resolution
that we not go into that country. Among post-war American
poets, only Randall Jarrell's "The Death of the Ball Turret
Gunner" spoke to me the way that many poems by Hayden did.

Similarly, in the early 1960s, Hayden wrote "Belsen, Day of
Liberation," drawing on his friendship with the Dutch
anthologist Rosey Pool, who had recounted to him her
experience in a Nazi concentration camp. Pool had told Hayden
about a young child observing the arrival of American troops in
a less debatable war than Vietnam:

Her parents and her dolls destroyed,
her childhood foreclosed,
she watched the foreign soldiers from
the sunlit window whose black bars

Were crooked crosses inked upon
her pallid face. "Liebchen,
Liebchen, you should be in bed...."

The reader senses that the child is weak with emaciation and
illness, an adult trying to protect her health even during the
moment of liberation, countless human tragedies surrounding
her, the individual and general lot under violence and war,

abuse and murder. The speaker's understatement and restraint from moralizing eloquently suggest and rely on the compassionate condemnation that all civilized people cannot but feel when presented with such an inhumane scene of suffering. The poet's compassion draws the reader into the poem, linking subtly the Nazi atrocities with the human failings evinced by the "crooked crosses" of the KKK.

In "Night, Death, Mississippi," Hayden's persona again appeals to the humanity of the reader when presented with the brutal and senseless violence of the hunting down of human beings, escaped slaves:

> Then we beat them, he said,
> beat them till our arms was tired
> and the big old chains
> messy and red.

The characterization in the language itself conjures up the ignorance that made such violence possible. No solipsistic postmodernism in Robert Hayden. I remember once his reading to me and laughing about a poem by Stanley Plumly, recounting Plumly's walking across the street to visit his grandma. Hayden gestured into the air, roaring, "Is that all?" No patience for the small world of the self, detached aestheticism, or doctrinaire nihilism, what Saul Bellow scathingly called "knee-jerk nihilism," indifference to life, in this world in which we have to live, struggling to stay afloat in what is too often a sea of interminable human evil and misery. Hayden's poetry is not the clichéd "poetry of witness," nor the accounts in the daily newspaper, but a profound meditation and exploration of the dehumanization and moral and spiritual vacuum that produce violence against other human beings. A pair of human eyes behind the mask of coke-bottle glasses peers out at the horror, seeking, demanding it mean something, that the toll of all the horror be taken account of and felt, felt by the reader with a human intimacy deep in the heart and soul, artfully suggesting,

"No more, no more. 'Raw head and bloodybones night.' No more." Deftly, Hayden's sensibility and craft carry the reader toward a higher stage of humanity. Consciously opposing Auden's stricture, Hayden believed, "Poetry does make something happen, for it changes sensibility" (*Collected Prose* 11). In such poems, Hayden taught and showed me the way to write about my own experience of modernity in my first book of poems, *Into the Ruins*.

Robert Hayden is one of the great American poets. When I think of the major modern poets W. B. Yeats, T. S. Eliot, W. H. Auden, and Czeslaw Milosz, I am compelled to recognize their comparative breadth and the fact that each also wielded a prose pen with which they studied the Tradition and plumbed its depths. Robert Hayden's prose is of a different nature, most of it composed of interviews. Talking with him once, he explained it to me by saying, "I've never really had any ideas about all that." I was shocked to hear him say that because I knew he had read widely in poetry and literature and taught various classes for decades. Yet his gift resides elsewhere, in poetry of remarkable language, clarity of vision, and deep insight into human character and motivation. I have always thought highly of what Professor Laurence Goldstein wrote in an article mourning his death in *The Detroit Free Press* on April 20, 1980: "Hayden ranked among the greatest of contemporary poets of any color." I still don't believe there's another American poet of his generation that achieved a body of poetry comparable in exquisite language, feeling, compassion, love, and universality of humane vision. His development over the decades was arduous and hard won, but his achievement shall last as long as people care about American literature and poetry. Thirty-three years after his death, Robert Hayden's poems have already demonstrated that they will be among those few to go forward into the centuries. Our presence here today indicates as much. "This man shall be remembered" long after his antagonists in the coterie of the Black Arts Movement are forgotten. Little fish swim in schools. Robert Hayden had the strength of character to stand alone.

In his interview in the Baha'i magazine *World Order*, during the US Bicentennial, Hayden carefully tells us what are the values he cherished. The importance of his choosing to do so in the pages of *World Order* cannot be overemphasized, leaving the critical implications to the discerning reader:

> How else shall we evolve except through commitment to transcendent values? It's not something which can be programmed, however; it's a matter of individual consciousness and conscience. Consider that in the past Americans have always been dissenters. Americans have never submitted for long to injustice. They have always gone to the defense of the underdog. Even in the days of slavery there were those people, like the Quakers, and there were the great men like Emerson and Thoreau, who laid it on the line and protested. Thoreau spent a night in jail rather than pay taxes to a slave-holding government. This is something which, during this Bicentennial period, we need to remember—that is, we have always been dissenters. There have always been among us people who have some vision of how things ought to be, and they have led the rest of us, the rest of the country, in the right direction (*CP* 85).

Unabashedly, unapologetically, Hayden has something he wants to communicate to the reader. Often after such meditations on horror, something he wants to tell us. Once, under a high window in Angell Hall, sunlight streaming in, in the very room in which Hayden said he had once sat in W. H. Auden's class, The Analysis of Poetry, I sat and heard him say it. Peering out towards the class, a book in one hand, mildly, quietly even, he tossed it out at us, the other hand grappling in the air, "Poetry has to have something to do with the transcendent." That is the ancient criterion of the highest art for all civilizations on this planet. Without any argument or followup, moving on to another topic, that was it. In his TV interview with Ron Scott, he stated it in the universal terms of the mystic, "There is something beyond and behind all that we do." I knew there and then in Angell Hall, and have never forgotten it, that I had heard words that were rarely spoken during the Age of Criticism, doctrinally tending to celebrate Nietzsche, Freud, and Marx, similar minds and thinkers, dehumanizing theories and academic sophistries. The very definition of an intelligent, educated person, East or West, has often come to be defined as one opposed to any form of transcendence, given the ever-ascending Myth of the secular Enlightenment, much tarnished now by the actual events of history, though widely ignored to our continuing woe, even suppressed.

Listening carefully to Hayden, he states in his interview with Denis Gendron, "I am often in despair" (*G* 161). Referring to *World Order*, for which he was poetry editor, and to a poem he was working on, "Sections will be left out for the magazine—some things I don't want to appear there," adding, "If I had not become a Baha'i (we have to attack this indirectly), I might have become a humanist." Talking about studying Baha'i in 1941, he says, in the *Collected Prose*, "My wife went to study groups more often than I did, and she still does, for that matter" (*CP* 110). Alluding broadly to authoritarian leaders, and behind the veil of art, to the Baha'i "councillors," who impose a very tight control over freedom of thought and speech, an authoritarianism that comes out of the worst in the Iranian Shiism underlying the Haifan Baha'i Faith, his poem "[American Journal]" refers to "The Counselors" to whom the persona must report back about his mission to earth:

The Counselors would never permit such barbarous
confusion   they know what is best for our sereni
ty . . .

                    . . . why should we sanction

86

old hypocrisies thus dissenters The Counse
lors would silence them

a decadent people The Counselors believe i
do not find them decadent a refutation not
permitted me

At times Hayden, and even Mrs. Hayden, would mention "counselors" they felt very worried about, for good reason as time has proven. Hayden is not addressing the decadence of Jacque Barzun's *From Dawn to Decadence* but more that of Sayyid Qutb of the Muslim Brotherhood, parallels of which exist among some Baha'is, especially some Iranians. Hayden was not a Baha'i fundamentalist and loathed literal-minded interpretations of the Baha'i writings and delighted in criticizing and caricaturing such Baha'is. In the poem "Night-Blooming Cereus," the persona, unobtrusively, slips in that the newly opened, beautiful flower is a "Lunar presence, / foredoomed, already dying," which is to say, belongs elsewhere than in this world, doomed from the beginning, that there are unequivocal signs the blossom shall not survive in this atmosphere, resonating like his sober words about Marcus Garvey's Back to Africa Movement, "With fantasies / of Ethiopia spreading her gorgeous wings." The setting off of "with fantasies" on a separate line powerfully and subtly drives home the point, enwrapped in Hayden's profoundly tragic vision. Trust the poem, not the poet.

Again, Hayden speaking in his interview with Gendron,

There is the part of my mind and the part of my being...that is convinced that there is transcendence, that there is a spiritual dimension and there is God, and that we do have obligations to God and that there is a divine plan for the world and so on. At the same time, there is the other side of me that finds it very hard to accept that, that finds it very hard to believe.... And I think that many artists are in this situation of believing and yet not being able somehow completely to surrender. And I have the feeling that, if I could completely surrender and be absolutely obedient and so on, everything in my life would fall into place. And yet I can't do it, and yet I can't do it. Well, some people are doing it, but I don't know whether artists are doing it.... Well, I am not a saint, and so there's no danger (*G* 158-160).

As he said to me once, "I have been half in and half out of *everything* all my life." In even more candid terms with me, alone in his study, he would quietly get up and close the door, and then say, "It has always been important to Erma that I remain a Baha'i." Repeatedly on other occasions, emphatically, "Why I continue to have anything to do with the Baha'i Faith, I do not know! I do not know!" Speaking of poets, Hayden said in his *World Order* interview, "We are the conscience of our people. I hope we never lose the freedom to write as we please—though we might."

After he died I continued to pack up his papers and dutifully delivered them to an archive of Mrs. Hayden's choosing. I remember sitting alone in his tiny study thinking of T. S. Eliot's line, "Leaving disordered papers in a dusty room." The room was no longer the same without him. And I recall Erma, perhaps in the role of loving wife, meaning well, telling me he had never been beaten as a child, though unbeknownst to her he himself had told me that he had. Similarly, as a caring wife will do, she always claimed much more involvement on his part with the Baha'i Faith, in Nashville and elsewhere, than he himself did. She referred to him once as believing much more strongly than she in the Baha'i Faith, though he always told me otherwise. They often were at loggerheads over religion. Mrs. Hayden had a number of Baha'i friends who always reminded me of Eric Hoffer's "true believers," whom Hayden always enjoyed mocking to me. Erma was an ardent Baha'i who occasionally evinced pronounced intolerance towards Baha'is who didn't tout the conventional pieties of the Haifan Baha'i administration.

Hayden appeared cowed at times by his wife in such regards, even as he treated the Baha'i administration with sarcasm and derision. He expressed similar views for the editorial board of *World Order*, finding them intellectually flaccid and conventional in literary and religious terms. Yet he very carefully honed and guarded his public persona. It is partly why he reacted against Gendron's dissertation, telling me he had threatened to sue Gendron if he published it, though Gendron denied it to me that it had ever happened. Hayden maintained he had spoken freely with Gendron but never imagined he would reveal it all publicly. Looking back, I believe it wasn't only Gendron's sexual revelations that worried him but also what the repercussions might have been of his nuanced criticism of Baha'i. He knew Baha'is could be harassed and excommunicated over very minor points of view or casually made remarks, extending then even to one's family. Some of the people whom Erma closely associated with were precisely the kind of people who were involved in rooting out heresy, excommunicating and "shunning" Baha'i "dissidents," a dirty word in the Baha'i lexicon.

Hayden once said, alluding to these matters and what he called The Problem, "I suppose everything will have to come out some day." I replied, "The world always deserves the truth. There can be no growth otherwise." Thirty-three years after the man's death, I don't believe personal obligation demands anything be hidden or swept under the rug. Quite the reverse. Everything is in the poems and the prose. Denis Gendron's dissertation and interview uniquely document Hayden's various struggles, are exactly what is now needed to help readers understand Hayden to a greater depth. To a significant degree, the world has caught up with Hayden on race, and his sexual battles need not be The Problem they used to be for a man of his generation.

In his long interview with Paul McCluskey in the *Collected Prose*, Hayden refers to "aspects of my life and experience I'm not about to share with the public—directly that is. In these poems I am rather speaking from behind the mask" (*CP* 161). He goes on to allow that he didn't have the "courage" and "self-confidence" to confront and reveal his "inmost" self but spoke through personae to tell the truth, like Emily Dickinson, who told "it slant." Perhaps his most direct statement is "I confess that as an artist I find it difficult to conform to the letter of the law" (*CP* 27). Ultimately his religious consciousness is in the broadest sense affirming "the humane, the universal, the potentially divine in the human creature" (*CP* 119-20). Comparable to Hayden's struggle with race, was his struggle to affirm what he said he always had: "I've always been a believer of sorts, despite periods of doubt and questioning. I've always had God-consciousness, as I call it, if not religion."

While one might think that Hayden is referring exclusively to the Baha'i Faith when he talks of "God-consciousness," his experience runs deeper and longer if again we listen carefully to what he has to say. For instance, in his TV interview with Ron Scott, he lightly slips in that he was very much involved with the Second Baptist Church when young, "much more than many think or realize," and was for a time training to be a missionary to Africa. He had once joked with me, "Can you imagine me a missionary to Africa? Howlingly funny!" His first book, *Heart Shape in the Dust*, usually comes up in terms of race and his involvement with the social struggles of the 1930s, but it also records Hayden had a sense of the spiritual even then, evolving further too with that theme throughout the years. One of his life insurance policies that I had occasion to see was with the Baptist church, Mrs. Hayden snatching it out of my hand, indignant that I had stumbled upon it. Hayden's spiritual life did not begin with his conversion to the Baha'i Faith, with his wife, in 1942. Nor did his becoming a Baha'i solve all of his personal problems. In many ways, I believe it made them worse, more unsolvable, hampering, I would argue, among other things, his acceptance of his sexuality. In 1975 Hayden told Gendron he felt blocked by something. I would argue it was his better judgement that something was amiss with the Baha'i Faith which doesn't sufficiently surface until the mid 1990s. In another sense Hayden finally confronts what blocks him in "The Tattoo Man," written late in the fall of 1979, finally accepting himself, despite the Baha'i doctrines that had confused him for much of his life, achieving an integration of being and healing that he had long sought.

To be clear, I am not saying Robert Hayden was not a Baha'i but that what he believed was the Baha'i Faith can now be seen as not entirely existing, reminiscent of W. B. Yeats's myth in his book *A Vision*. Yeats had struggled for, but never achieved, Unity of Being, seeking it throughout *A Vision* and his writing. For all his phantasmagoria, he could not create or renew a convincing vision, a Unity of Being. I believe *A Vision* can now be achieved on the moon, or from the moon, for our time has seen and felt the impact of the great symbol, Mother Earth, her circling embrace, as her arms wrap around us, a celestial Rose Image, a transcendent image in the universe. Viewing our homeland from space, who can doubt that Unity of Being returns?

Hayden learned this, too, from Yeats, a myth that Hayden did not have to write *entirely* for himself. Hayden's universal myth was a turn to seeking divine grace and mercy, symbolically in many poems, but not one including for Hayden the kind of things that have transpired during the last decade and a half in the religion. As I wrote in my 1983 essay in *World Order* (Summer), "Re-centering: The Turning of the Tide and Robert Hayden," I still believe he's the first American poet to begin to realize there's a way out of the anomie of modernity, through universality, and a profound change of sensibility, not ultimately narrowly defined as an exclusive Baha'i box. We human beings, our thinking so narrow and restrictive, as soon as we "organize," in the supposed best interest of others, "religious" or "secular," every "box" failing sooner or later, often with much woe before we realize it. To my mind, the whole modern assortment of cardboard boxes, whether traditional institutional "religion" or the Enlightenment myth and its offspring, are crumbling all around us, unable to hold together and do justice to the contents of the psyche, protect us from our own worst passions and assumptions, crippling fragmentation our daily bread and dilemma. It's not an easy task to confront all that and suggest a modest reassessment, not utopian hubris, but it seems that every sign continues to demonstrate how urgent it is that we human beings achieve it. What but universality offers hope in the face of all the movements clamoring for exclusivism, in one form or another? What have we lived into around the globe if not the rich and fertile pluralism of universality?

Similarly, heroically, Hayden maintained that there is no such thing as white poetry, nor Black poetry, just American poetry. The same can be said for "Baha'i poetry." Ironically, the situation has developed in terms of Robert Hayden's being a Baha'i that is exactly analogous to what happened regarding his views on race. He had found himself increasingly having to explain he was a poet, not a racial propagandist to people who could not conceive of an artist as anything else. His being a Baha'i has resulted in some unsophisticated readers thinking all the problems and doubts of human existence were resolved for the rest of eternity for the "Baha'i poet." The living, breathing man, with all his struggles, is much more worth reading than the plaster Baha'i saint. Hayden's poetry is much more sophisticated and nuanced, questioning the nature of reality and whether and how we can know it, to what extent such knowledge is even possible. Robert Hayden speaks on many levels about transcendence and *his* Baha'i Faith.

There are now several Bahai denominations, with major upheavals, as I've alluded to, taking place only after his death in 1980, especially beginning with the mid 1980s in the United Kingdom, with the harassing of the British scholar Denis MacEoin, driving him out of the religion, into the mid 1990s, with the driving out of several American scholars and writers either into silence or withdrawal, as with Professor Juan Cole of the University of Michigan, reported in his Biography on juancole.com (search "Baha'i"). In 2008 fifteen Bahai scholars and writers were declared in the prestigious London scholarly journal *Religion*, by the Baha'i administrator and medical doctor Moojan Momen, to be "apostates," Juan Cole and myself, with a few others, selected out among them for special treatment, much of the story of which can be found in my book *Letters from the American Desert* and on my Baha'i Censorship website, both of which present the early history of the Bahai Movement in the United States that I believe Robert Hayden never knew about and was unaware of the extent to which it had been turned in the direction of control and power, like most Baha'is of the largest denomination, even today. What Juan Cole has suggested in his book *Modernity and the Millennium* (Cambridge University Press 1998) and in numerous articles, as the theocratic fundamentalism of the Baha'i Faith, has become undeniable since Robert Hayden's death, shockingly evident in its attempt in the U. S. Federal Court of Northern Illinois, from 2006 through 2010, to destroy three other Bahai denominations.[3] Although Hayden once stated "The Baha'i Faith is about the only organized body I can stand," it may have largely been because the Machiavellian thinking of some of its administrators was more carefully concealed during his lifetime, and he took it too much at face value, not questioning it enough, deferring to his wife for domestic harmony, though finding in it a much needed personal and literary myth.

---

[3](a) fglaysher.com/bahaicensorship (b) "Marginality and Apostasy in the Baha'i Community," Moojan Momen, in *Religion* 37 2007. 187–209. For my "A Response to Takfir," see "Challenging apostasy: Responses to Moojan Momen's 'Marginality and Apostasy in the Baha'i Community.'" *Religion* 38 No 4 2008. 384-393. (c) The Oral Argument before, and the Opinion of, the United States District Court for the Northern District of Illinois and the United States Court of Appeals for the Seventh Circuit are available on www.ca7.uscourts.gov and elsewhere on the Internet. Case No. 08-2306. 2006-2010.

No one can speak for a dead man, but I can say that I believe that the man I knew would never have tolerated or condoned such acts, would have been aghast at what has become of the religion, largely behind the granite facade. Robert Hayden must not be allowed to be coopted into any position that remotely suggests he would have approved of such injustice and fanaticism or used to justify such claims and practices, as has been implicitly done on his Wikipedia page, if one follows deep enough the links, firmly in control of Bahai fundamentalists for over a decade. In literature we know that the career and writing of a poet can be used by scholars, critics, and other writers for purposes that the poet would never have approved. Robert Hayden's poetry is too important and vital to American literature to be enlisted anachronistically in the proselytizing and support of an organization that has increasingly become antithetical to much of what Hayden tells us is most important to him—justice and human dignity, freedom and liberty of conscience, democratic principles, and the transcendence that he found in the universal Divine.

In the end, we have Hayden's impeccable art, as in his Yeatsian meditation on Whistler's "The Peacock Room," which he called one of his "most important poems" (*CP* 125), where Hayden artfully writes, "briefly I shelter":

> What is art?
> What is life?
> What the Peacock Room?
> Rose-leaves and ashes drift
> its portals, gently spinning toward
> a bronze Bodhisattva's ancient smile.

Aristotle's *Poetics* and Epic Poetry

As of May 27, 2011, I've revised each book of *The Parliament of Poets* through Book VII, since finishing the full rough draft of the entire epic in early February. Past the half way mark of revision feels very good and inspires me to want to push on through the rest of it during the next several weeks, perhaps before the end of the summer, a readable draft of the entire book.

It was as a young poet, holed up in some rental room or house, choosing consciously and painfully to live in poverty in order to have the time to study and write, in Detroit or in the country, none of my family or friends understanding what I was doing, that I first read Aristotle's *Poetics*, some thirty-five years ago. I reread it many times, or parts of it, going back to it through the years. It is the touchstone of the literary art.

Aristotle was right, in so many ways, nowhere more than when he wrote, in the *Poetics*, a useful critical work, rightly revered by poets for millennia, unlike the vapid theories that have been for decades the bane of American and English poetry:

> So from these considerations it is evident that the poet should be a maker of his plots more than of his verses, insofar as he is a poet by virtue of his imitations and what he imitates is actions. (Tr. Gerald F. Else)

The plot presents the most formidable challenge to an epic poet, selecting the incidents and structuring the chain of events, as well as the perspective on them. After long decades of pondering and searching for the Idea, a dream in the night can come as from another realm.

Saul Bellow, in his 1987 Bennington College address *Summations,* refers to Osip Mandelstam's comment that "a worldview is a tool and instrument, like a hammer in the hands of a stonemason." The average reader, Bellow goes on to say, looks always for the worldview, thinking it is everything, filing away the summation, its neat, little abstractions. I would say, many writers, too, make the mistake of fixating upon the worldview, the struggle to achieve an understanding of one's experience that is not derivative from the prevailing one, a mere reflection of the already-thought-and-written, though so much writing merely reflects the fads of the academy and literati. Mandelstam and Bellow are right. It is the hammer in the hand of the genuine artist or poet. Painfully, laboriously forged, the tool, the Idea, once achieved, is no longer to the poet what is of first importance. The work of art, beyond the abstractions and the banalities of "a worldview," reigns supreme, leads to new states of consciousness that cannot be summed up. They are what art is about. Art transcends worldview.

In contrast, one thinks of Ezra Pound's plotless, rambling attempt at epic, and other modern efforts, without exception mere series of poems, pastiche, or mock epics, narrative as epic, though there is no reason a universal epic for our time cannot include humor and delight along with wisdom. The great epics, East and West, need not bind our hands but guide them.

Epic song raises a new vision for the people, for the culture, helps renew and clarify what is the deepest, most profound vision that is already forming, independent of the poet and the poem, global now, inviting people to a new way forward. The very nature of epic poetry is that it reassesses the prevailing order and articulates a fresh vision of life, already rising on the foundations of the past.

Before there was art, before the modern panoply, there was worship of the Unseen Essence, and human beings of all tribes, in every aspect of their lives, expressed, recorded, honored, intimated, found metaphors for their experience of what the Lakota Indians, for one, called Wakan Tanka, the Great Mystery. But we've been colleged. We'd never fall for that. After all, what was Marx and Freud and the great Enlightenment all about? What were they for? It's either one or the other. One is either an educated person or one is not.

Beyond sophistry, Aristotle observes, "imitation comes naturally to us, and melody and rhythm too"; talking of already ancient epic, "the soberer spirits were imitating noble actions and the actions of noble persons," which I have always read as the rare qualities of character exemplifying humanity at its best, ideally, for instance, as with Dante's persona, his longing for Beatrice.

Dante and Virgil, among my masters, were often on my mind, in terms of structure, and so much else. Dante's cantos made me realize that I could combine the twelve books of Virgil and Milton with his form, usually with three or four cantos per book, though I chose not to denote them as such. I think, too, Dante's canto works in terms of the attention span of readers, giving relief, occasionally, when needed, allowing modulation.

Further, too, I should say, the language of an epic, in our *lingua franca*, not only the length, must be carefully chosen if it is to have any chance of reaching a global readership, of speaking to people around the globe. While not condescending to their audience, the greatest epics were simple and direct, seeking to communicate with their listeners and readers.

Of the embellishment of poetic style, Aristotle writes,

> But by far the most important thing is to be good at metaphor. This is the only part of the job that cannot be learned from others; on the contrary it is a token of high native gifts, for making good metaphors depends on perceiving the likenesses in things.

Similarly, anthropologists have argued precisely that the distinguishing attribute of *Homo sapiens* is the ability for symbolic thought and metaphor. I would add metaphor comprises many levels of language and form, shading into structural devices and image, grounded in sensibility, temperament, and in that regard Aristotle is correct that metaphor can't be learned, but lived, lived into, is a way of thinking. The prerequisites for that journey presuppose a search of the highest order.

Somewhere in my mid-twenties, I began to train my mind to the task of writing an epic poem. It became the filter through which I passed everything I read and thought. Can I use this? Will it help me? I could merely sniff a book and detect whether it was worthwhile or not, glance at an article and know if it would repay reading. I learned to carry in my head those facts and details, characters and allusions, that grabbed me by the soul and shook me to the depths. I knew they alone were worthy of epic song. All else I brushed off, no matter how highly thought of by others. The grist for my mill accumulated. The burden of what I was carrying became immense. Even earlier in life, I had begun to realize that I would not find much help in the university and would have to travel and face the blank page alone.

Epic problems and their solutions lead to mimesis, imitation of things, in one of three ways: "the way they were or are; the way they are said or thought to be; the way they ought to be." Homer and Sophocles set the best example by "portraying people as they ought to be." Epic poetry can do no less than strive to approach their standard and is ultimately judged by its own failure and success.

Aristotle's *Poetics* is as universally applicable to the greatest epics of Eastern and Asian literature as it is to those of the Western Greco-Roman and English tradition, applicable to all of world literature.

Decadence, East and West

The scholar Jacques Barzun provides our initial definition of decadence, in his brilliant survey of intellectual history, *From Dawn to Decadence: 1500 to the Present, 500 years of Western Cultural Life* (2000): "All that is meant by decadence is 'falling off.'" His discussion ranges over Western art, music, religion, and literature, documenting and critiquing the many figures, changes, and evolutions up to the reigning vision of our time, which he succinctly epitomizes while defending the term of his assessment: "When people accept futility and the absurd as normal, the culture is decadent. The term is not a slur; it is a technical label." Barzun goes on to explain how one can identify when a culture declines into decadence:

> How does the historian know when Decadence sets in? By the open confessions of malaise, by the search in all directions for a new faith or faiths.... To secular minds, the old ideals look outworn or hopeless and practical aims are made into creeds sustained by violent acts....

From this perspective, modern Western culture has been in free-fall for over a hundred years, arguably even longer. Whether high or low, such is the story of Western civilization, and, to the extent that it became modern civilization, its decadence has long been passed around the world, into the vitals of every regional civilization on the face of the earth. Together, we have all sunk into the dark pit of cynicism, frivolity, and despair, "fallen off" into nihilism.

By now, the story is an old one. We all know it by rote. Artists, poets, philosophers, and scholars have rubbed it deep into our souls for decades, as have the media on their lower cultural levels, print, radio, and film. The Dark Vision is the Truth of Life. Modernity has intoned with Nietzsche, "God is dead." Nietzsche's transvaluation was a devaluation that has manifested itself in the streets of modernity, debasing what is best in the Enlightenment into nihilism. The theaters of the absurd have dramatized it in endlessly boring detail. All kinds of crud have been smeared on museum walls lest we fail to see it. Cacophony has droned it into our heads. No one of intellectual respectability dare deny it, East or West. As Lionel Trilling confided to his diary in 1948, we have become "assimilated to the literal contents of the art we contemplate [so] that our contemplation of cruelty will not make us humane but cruel; that the reiteration of the badness of our spiritual condition will make us consent to it." We become the "adversary culture." Such are among the *a priori* assumptions and propaganda of modern decadence.

Many have observed that the decline into moral and social decadence has been accompanied, paradoxically, by the dramatically opposite phenomenon of exponential scientific and technological advance, unprecedented in the history of humanity. As the poet Czeslaw Milosz noted in 1999, in "A Dialogue of Cultures" in *New Perspective Quarterly*:

> A race is on between disintegration and construction. And each aspect is related to the other. The advances of science and technology have further eroded the religious imagination. For that reason, believers and non-believers are in the same boat because the quality of the imagination does not depend upon what you believe, but how that imagination is conditioned by technological civilization and science. ...when the world is deprived of clear-cut outlines, of up and down, of good and evil, it succumbs to a peculiar nihilization.

The splitting apart of science and religion, throughout modernity, has increasingly widened the gap between humane, spiritual principles and beliefs and the relentlessly stripped-down nihilism that has firmly sunk its grip into the soul of man. From the withdrawal after the Wars of Religion in Europe, typified by Thomas Sprat's famous 1722 account, in

100

The History of the Royal Society, of scientists withdrawing into their own realm, the divide has widened, carrying modern culture ever further away from the moderating influence of the moral and spiritual Imagination, constituting a decline into an ever-worsening dehumanization and alienation from the deepest springs of human nature. When humanists, such as Barzun and Milosz, make this criticism, it is not of science and technology, that is, systematic knowledge and the study of the natural world and its application, but of the hubris involved in imagining such valuable material advances render unnecessary a compatible development in moral and spiritual growth, required for humanity to protect itself from the misuse of its own increased knowledge and discoveries. All of which explains the frequent contemporary sense, often felt in our time, of things being extremely complex and out of control, in a frightening state of affairs and decline, despite the highly sophisticated development of material culture.

In "Questions for the Third Millennium," in 1991, Milosz provided a significant insight into the evolving way out of the malaise, the resolution of the severing of the unity of being and consciousness into artificially separated realms, writing, that Quantum Mechanics,

> ...restores the mind to its role of a co-creator in the fabric of reality. This favors a shift from belittling man as an insignificant speck in the immensity of galaxics to regarding him again as the main actor in the universal drama—which is a vision proper to every religion (Blake's Divine Humanity, Adam Kadmon of the Cabbalah, Logos-Christ of the Christian denominations).

I would add all the global forms of transcendence and spirituality to his list, the Upanishads and the Bhagavad Gita, Buddhism, Daoism, Confucianism, along with The Dreaming and the other indigenous forms of the human meeting the Divine. The rocky road of modern nihilism has cleared the ground for all humanity to come together before the universal meaning and affirmation of human existence, in all humility and awe, science and the humanities, before the Unknowable Essence that governs all of us and the cosmos.

The Bengali writer Nirad C. Chaudhuri, in *Thy Hand, Great Anarch!: India, 1921–1952*, bemoaning the decadence of Bengal and Hindi-speaking northern India, England and the West, including Canada and the United States, where he lived for a short time, spending the last twenty-five years of his life in England, wrote,

> But even the highest intellects of today do not see the darkness as I see it. They do not admit that there is any cultural or social decadence. This is due in the first instance to the insensibility to decadence which any historical movement of decadence always creates.... In such ages the general habit of intellectuals is to refuse to face all realities, and their incurable disposition is to impose a pattern of words on all reality. This disease is universal in the world of today (962).

Given his global perspective on decadence, Chaudhuri probes profoundly into the nature of the last hundred years and our continuing plight. For even as a way out of it can now be discerned, as culture has increasingly evolved towards universality, the keys of the kingdom, so to speak, are often in the hands of intellectuals who bar the way through the door, to a new and healthier stage of civilization, healthier than smugly self-righteous, fanatical nihilism. Chaudhuri's most brilliant insight into modernity was that "The really dangerous aspect of decadence in human communities is the insensibility to it which it always creates." After the pathetic little piety that "God is dead," no denial is more common among the worst type of radically politicized intellectuals, especially in American universities, than the rejection of any critique of social and cultural decadence. To allow such an assertion would open the door to morality, and that was supposedly slain by Nietzsche along with God. Better to have "a pattern of words," empty abstractions and discourse than anything approaching a moral and spiritual understanding of the human being.

Unlike the crowd of intellectuals whom Chaudhuri criticizes, sycophants for the most part who mindlessly mumble the platitudes of received nihilism, Philip Rieff, an outstanding intellectual and critic of Freud and modern psychology, in his book *My Life among the Deathworks*, critiques modern Western art and nihilism, writing a highly sophisticated and nuanced analysis of modernity, in which he uses a scaffolding of terms based on first, second, and third world paradigms, the last referring not to the developing world but to the post-Christian and post-religious one of nihilism:

> What the third world needs, but refuses to admit. There is a desperate need for an elite that carries an interdictory sense, a reading elite that carries illuminative certainties. Third world elites will not allow the development, or redevelopment, of such a reading elite. Our new age elite cannot and will not tolerate such authority (195).

Essentially agreeing with Chaudhuri, Rieff emphasizes that the way is barred through the conventional doors of the academy and its associated cultural institutions, to which I'd add, its publications, whether book or journal, including wider circulation magazines, such as *The New York Times Book Review*, *The New York Review of Books*, *Harper's*, *TLS*, *The Guardian*, and other such monopolizing arbiters of cultural opinion in the United States, the United Kingdom, and elsewhere. I recall that Czeslaw Milosz often criticized American small press literary magazines for their intellectual and spiritual vacuity. It was in the early 1990s that their moral and spiritual sterility, along with piles of rejection slips, led me to decide to stop submitting my writing to them, as well as the Catholic and

Christian journals in which I had published, realizing I didn't belong in any of them either.

Basically for the same reasons, some years later, I resigned in 1996 from teaching at Oakland University. It was with the deepest sense of revulsion and loathing that I had come to understand the American university was not capable of respecting and sustaining anyone, including myself, who believed in the moral and spiritual nature of the human being. I chose to follow what I considered the way of all the great masters, solitude, trusting that God would somehow open the door. I affirm it was the wisest thing that I've ever done.

This entire process of decline into decadence was noted and expounded by the ancients, foremost among commentators, by Plato, in *The Republic*, written approximately in 380 BCE, about twenty-five years after the collapse of Athenian democracy into tyranny, wherein Socrates describes the "luxurious city" in a "fevered state," compared with a healthy one:

> It is not merely the origin of a city, it seems, that we are considering but the origin of a luxurious city…. But if it is your pleasure that we contemplate also a fevered state, there is nothing to hinder. For there are some, it appears, who will not be contented with this sort of fare or with this way of life, but couches will have to be added thereto and tables and other furniture, yes, and relishes and myrrh and incense and girls and cakes—all sorts of all of them. And the requirements we first mentioned, houses and garments and shoes, will no longer be confined to necessities, but we must set painting to work and embroidery, and procure gold and ivory and similar adornments, must we not? (Bollingen edition)

Socrates' point is that in the decadent "luxurious state" the emphasis has all been placed on the material, far beyond the necessities of life. Those who "will not be contented" desire more and more things. Much later, in Book IX, Socrates asks his interlocutor, "is it not generally true that" men who are "concerned with the service of the body partake less of truth and reality than those that serve the soul?" Expanding on this question, Socrates summarizes for Glaucon,

> Then those who have no experience of wisdom and virtue but are ever devoted to feastings and that sort of thing are swept downward, it seems, and back again to the center, and so sway and roam to and fro throughout their lives, but they have never transcended all this and turned their eyes to the true upper region nor been wafted there, nor ever been really filled with real things, nor ever tasted stable and pure pleasure, but with eyes ever bent upon the earth and heads bowed down over their tables they feast like cattle, grazing and copulating, ever greedy for more of these delights, and in their greed kicking and butting one another with horns and hoofs of iron they slay one another in sateless avidity, because they are vainly striving to satisfy with things that are not real the unreal and incontinent part of their souls.
> You describe in quite oracular style, Socrates, said Glaucon, the life of the multitude.

Socrates further explains how the law courts become corrupt, undermining the state and leading to tyranny. Decline into the luxurious city produces its rotten fruit. Men seek satisfaction in "things that are not real," have lost touch with who and what they really are.

The Italian Giambattista Vico, writing in the 18th Century, in his book *The New Science*, noted the same process of decline into luxury and the decadence of "each man thinking only of his own private interests," and ultimately returning society through the choice of self-destruction to "primitive simplicity":

> But if the peoples are rotting in that ultimate civil disease and cannot agree on a monarch from within, and are not

conquered and preserved by better nations from without, then providence for their extreme ill has its extreme remedy at hand. For such peoples, like so many beasts, have fallen into the custom of each man thinking only of his own private interests and have reached the extreme of delicacy, or better of pride, in which like wild animals they bristle and lash out at the slightest displeasure. Thus no matter how great the throng and press of their bodies, they live like wild beasts in a deep solitude of spirit and will, scarcely any two being able to agree since each follows his own pleasure and caprice. By reasons of all this, providence decrees that, through obstinate factions and desperate civil wars, they shall turn their cities into forests and the forests into dens and lairs of men. In this way, through long centuries of barbarism, rust will consume the misbegotten subtleties of malicious wits that have turned them into beasts made more inhuman by the barbarism of reflection than the first men had been made by the barbarism of sense. For the latter displayed a generous savagery, against which one could defend oneself or take flight or be on one's guard; but the former, with a base savagery, under soft words and embraces, plots against the life and fortune of friends and intimates. Hence peoples who have reached this point of premeditated malice, when they receive this last remedy of providence and are thereby stunned and brutalized, are sensible no longer of comforts, delicacies, pleasures, and pomp, but only of the sheer necessities of life. And the few survivors in the midst of an abundance of the things necessary for life naturally become sociable and, returning to the primitive simplicity of the first world of peoples, are again religious, truthful, and faithful. Thus providence brings back among them the piety, faith, and truth which are the natural foundations of justice as well as the graces and beauties of the eternal order of God" (424, trs Bergin and Fisch).

To emphasize, Vico continues, that it was "choice" that brought all this about, "not fate," an act of the mind, done with "intelligence": "That which did all this was mind, for men did it with intelligence; it was not fate, for they did it by choice; not chance, for the results of their always so acting are perpetually the same" (425). He concludes that "Hence, if religion is lost among the peoples, they have nothing left to enable them to live in society: no shield of defense, nor means of counsel, nor basis of support, nor even a form by which they may exist in the world at all" (426). It is that loss that has led to "each man thinking only of his own private interests," in the "pride" of his own heart, lashing out at others, as the entire civilization descends again further into barbarism.

Writing largely of the cities and desert dynasties of the Maghrib, Northern Africa, the great Islamic historian Ibn Khaldun makes much the same observations, in the 14th Century, in *An Introduction to History*:

> Senility is a chronic disease that cannot be cured or made to disappear because it is something natural, and natural things do not change.... Many a politically conscious person among the people of the dynasty becomes alert to it and notices the symptoms and causes of senility that have affected his dynasty. He considers it possible to make that senility disappear. Therefore, he takes it upon himself to repair the dynasty and relieve its temper of senility. He supposes that it resulted from shortcomings or negligence on the part of former members. This is not so. These things are natural to the dynasty. Customs that have developed prevent him from repairing it. Customs are like a second nature....
>
> Group feeling has often disappeared (when the dynasty has grown senile), and pomp has taken the place it occupied in the souls of men. Now, when in addition to the weakening of group feeling, pomp, too, is discontinued, the subjects grow audacious vis-a-vis the

dynasty. Therefore, the dynasty shields itself by holding on to pomp as much as possible, until everything is finished....

At the end of a dynasty, there often appears some show of power that gives the impression that the senility of the dynasty has been made to disappear. It lights up brilliantly just before it is extinguished, like a burning wick the flame of which leaps up brilliantly a moment before it goes out, giving the impression it is just starting to burn, when in fact it is going out (245-6, tr Rosenthal).

Later, Ibn Khaldun brings these themes together and concludes,

From all these customs, the human soul receives a multiple stamp that undermines its religion and worldly well-being....

All this is caused by excessive sedentary culture and luxury. They corrupt the city generally in respect to business and civilization. Corruption of the individual inhabitants is the result of painful and trying efforts to satisfy the needs caused by their luxury customs; the result of the bad qualities they have acquired in the process of satisfying those needs; and of the damage the soul suffers after it has obtained them. Immorality, wrongdoing, insincerity, and trickery, for the purpose of making a living in a proper or an improper manner, increase among them. The soul comes to think about making a living, to study it, and to use all possible trickery for the purpose. People are now devoted to lying, gambling, cheating, fraud, theft, perjury, and usury. Because of the many desires and pleasures resulting from luxury, they are found to know everything about the ways and means of immorality, they talk openly about it and its causes, and give up all restraint in discussing it, even among relatives and close female relations, where the Bedouin attitude requires modesty and avoidance of obscenities. They also know everything about fraud and deceit, which they employ to defend themselves against the possible use of force against them and against the punishment expected for their evil deeds. Eventually, this becomes a custom and trait of character with most of them, except those whom God protects (285-287).

Ibn Khaldun shares with Plato and Vico all the classic observations of decadence in a civilization: luxury, the excessive desire for and valuing of material goods, leading to moral corruption of the individual and society, the loss of spiritual qualities, characteristics, and morals, that safeguard the individual and social order, and the collapse into disorder, violence, and barbarism. The Greek *polis* or city, the Italian city-state, the Islamic dynasties, have become the world, with all our global problems and dilemmas leading back to the corrupt and suppurating soul, wandering lost, in the secular and nihilistic landscape and spiritual vacuum of modernity.

All modern people, in Jacques Barzun's sense, have "fallen" into decadence. Christians are not exempt, nor the members of any other faith, many of whom are caught, to varying degrees, in various "backward," fundamentalist movements and flights into fantasies of by-gone days, evangelicals and otherwise, none of which are tenable in the modern world. All such movements are a sign of decadence. The fullness of human experience cannot be repudiated and result in a satisfying vision for our time. The "graying out" of the mainline Christian denominations demonstrate decadence as well, by construing Christ's teachings in terms of doctrines, what Tolstoy called "sorcery," and tending to the flock of plutocrats that often support them, not the poor Christ cared about, broadly, the people. Christian fundamentalism and fanaticism are essentially rearguard nihilistic flights into the past. Humankind can only go forward, together, into the permanent pluralism of our quotidian experience, of what is universally human and Divine. From the moon, together, we can see it.

Like all the great religions, too, in modern times, Islam has fallen into fanaticism and fantasy, mistaking a backward, retrograde movement for the real thing. Modern nihilism has taken many forms, with Islam having its own. Islamo-fascism and authoritarianism is a form of nihilism that the great Sufi poets would have repudiated. They would never have mistaken it as a vehicle in which they could have traveled toward the Simorgh. The famous hadith states, "Seek knowledge even unto China," but much of Islam stopped following that injunction centuries ago, as it has fallen, for some, not all Muslims, into fanaticism and terrorism. Religious violence is the surest sign of decadence. Many observers, historians, and others have remarked that very little of scientific worth or innovation has been produced in Islamic countries for a very long time. I would argue, too, as some Muslims have said, the majority are closer to the Sufis than the Wahhabis, though the majority marginalize the Sufis. To that extent, what has happened to Islam in the modern world has also been a global decline into decadence. Hinduism, too, has had its backward conservative movements into the past, as an attempt to deal with the modernity that Milosz identifies as "peculiar" to our time.

The Quran (9:29) says,

> Fight those who believe not in Allah, nor the Last Day, nor hold that forbidden which hath been forbidden by Allah and His Messenger, nor acknowledge the Religion of Truth, from among the People of the Book, until they pay the Jizya [tax] with willing submission and feel themselves subdued.

There are many other similar verses. They're well known to anyone who actually reads the Quran. For the fanatics, and some moderate Muslims, that's Islam. And it cannot be soft-pedaled. Nothing discredits Islam more than its reduction to a political power symbol, as Ibn Khaldun recognized, and the use of violence and terrorism in an attempt to install it. The great jurists who developed and practiced the principles of "ijtihad," a moderately balanced interpretation of the Quran, did, have, and would condemn such violence, lack of compassion, and a sense of the historical moment. Their sense of the fullness of the text of the Quran would note, "Let there be no compulsion in religion"; "Unto you your religion, unto me my religion"; "God has respited the People of the Book"; "If God had pleased, He would have made you all one people. But He has done otherwise." Hearing only one part of the voice of God in the Quran turns it into an idol, and the individual into a decadent fanatic, seeking through pride and violence to impose his distorted interpretation on others.

In his "Farewell Address" of 1796, President George Washington spoke in a well-known passage about the positive role that religion plays in civilization:

> Of all the dispositions and habits which lead to political prosperity, religion and morality are indispensable supports. In vain would that man claim the tribute of patriotism who should labor to subvert these great pillars of human happiness, these firmest props of the duties of men and citizens. The mere politician, equally with the pious man, ought to respect and to cherish them. A volume could not trace all their connections with private and public felicity. Let it simply be asked where is the security for property, for reputation, for life, if the sense of religious obligation desert the oaths, which are the instruments of investigation in courts of justice? And let us with caution indulge the supposition that morality can be maintained without religion. Whatever may be conceded to the influence of refined education on minds of peculiar structure, reason and experience both forbid us to expect that national morality can prevail in exclusion of religious principle.

Similarly, Vico emphasized the role of religion in inspiring and sustaining morality and social order:

> For religions alone can bring the peoples to do virtuous works by appeal to their feelings, which alone move men to perform them; and the reasoned maxims of the philosophers concerning virtue are of use only when employed by a good eloquence for kindling the feelings to do the duties of virtue (426).

Comparatively, the cloying cliques of modernity have their hands clasped over their ears, like Muslim fanatics, shutting out all voices other than the received wisdom of what Saul Bellow once so rightly called "knee-jerk nihilism." The deeply felt awe before the sublime, the experience of the divine, is one thing, while the emotional impulse to fanaticism and persecution is another. The former, properly understood and guided, leads to humility, selflessness, and service before other human beings, because one who has experienced the transcendent realizes others, too, are a creation of the Divine, to be cherished and nurtured. The emotional fanaticism that leads to persecution, whether religious or secular, is based on a sense of exclusivism run amok, that denies the humanity of the other, including the others' unique interior consciousness and spirituality. Along those lines, the emotions and "reason" of the officially atheist regimes of Marxism and communism demonstrated their inability to respect the individual and responded by murdering over a hundred million people during the 20th Century.

Part of modernity's litany is that religious feeling and belief are always wrong, arrogantly failing or refusing to recognize the vast extent to which "Enlightenment" thinking and its offspring, such as Marxism, can and has led to cruelty, violence, and oppression. The notion that stripping humanity of "religion" will produce Utopia is woefully unlessoned by history. Another one of modernity's reflex actions, which works against its finding a resolution to our modern problems, before it is too late on so many fronts, is its tendency to react like a bull, confronted with a red cape, when it hears words such as "religion," "spiritual," and "God." It thinks it understands the meaning of those words, when it doesn't, having lost the meaning, often generations ago, and rejects making any effort to understand that perhaps significantly new definitions are being used or have evolved, instead of the caricatures it prefers. All of this is part of why we live in such an endangered moment of world history, armed to the teeth with enough megatonnage to easily kill more than a billion people, without the moral, humanizing restraint that religion cultivates. All sides, as currently conceived and constituted, are inadequate for providing an alternative to such carnage and a common basis or vision for a secure social order.

Beginning with I. A. Richards in the 1920s through the New Critics and onward through post-structuralism and Deconstruction, the Age of Criticism has served well neither the literary Tradition nor the culture. During the last thirty years, the American academy has often betrayed the deepest principles of the Tradition and of civilization. Every imaginable form of intellectual decline, decadence, and banality has long been the daily gruel served up for its students, debasing and corrupting the entire culture, spreading around the globe. Critics do not own the Tradition. No one has appointed them. Zeus has not handed down a graven tablet, passing, to Oxford and Cambridge, Harvard and Yale, or any other university, title to the Tradition. The *coup d'état* is the most apt trope for the Age of Criticism. When scholars of even the ability of Harold Bloom imagine they choose the inheritors of the Tradition, it becomes clear how lost in the wilderness they really are. Poets, writers, and artists, ultimately readers, are the fiduciary agents of the Tradition. Critics have too often lost and forgotten what their role is in the culture, secondary, and should go back to the 2,500-year-old Berlin Painter's Rhapsode Amphora, meditating long and hard, on their knees, in their offices, begging the gods to help them remember and understand, discern and relearn the duty and reciprocity imaged there.

The meta-narrative of the Enlightenment has often led the culture astray, down cynical, divisive, Balkanizing, appallingly violent and ill-begotten paths. Civilization on this planet remains woefully threatened by the nihilism that too often accompanies the Myth of the Enlightenment. The Myth often has taken the culture in the wrong direction. Together, from the moon, we can see the way beyond the Enlightenment and postmodernity. Fortunately, perhaps, the Internet and Post-Gutenberg publishing have been developed by science and technology just at the moment when the spirit requires new channels through which to flow, circumventing the decadent bastions of much of the American university, especially its vitiated English departments, and its corrupt cultural institutions and influence, global now, toward a fourth world of universality.

Art and poetry's deepest answer to these problems is the hard, slow, arduous evolution of the soul, the thinking underlying the action and inaction of people and society. I fully understand that such an answer can seem inadequate to those who feel there is an urgent need now to change society, whatever society, overnight, especially young people arguing, and often rightly, that older generations are stuck in the mud, unwilling to make the necessary changes, and feeling impatient with such suggestions. I can only argue politicization and polarization lead to violence, and violence is always wrong, causing tragically more suffering and want for the masses of people. As hard as it might be to believe, especially these days, the example set by such leaders and writers as Tolstoy, Gandhi, Martin Luther King, Nelson Mandela, many Indian poets and religious figures, who emphasized peaceful evolution towards change and spiritual development of the individual soul, a change of heart and thought, leading to a change in action, and eventually impacting social structure and practice, remains the best, most peaceful, humane way for peoples to find and set a new direction for society, global now. Not easy, the changing of human consciousness, but the past is replete with many examples of how it was successfully done in the past. I believe it is still possible, all the more so now, on both the national and global levels. We stand on the cusp of such change, in the midst of it, and I believe peoples all around the world sense the need for it, are groping for a way to move forward. Artists can, will, and are already playing crucial roles in such an evolution of the soul.

Pitirim A. Sorokin was a sociologist at Harvard during the early half of the 20th Century who had lived through and participated in the Russian Revolution, eventually emigrating to the West. That experience gave him a unique insight into the problems and decadence of modernity. Writing in 1941 in *The Crisis of Our Age*:

> The present trouble represents the disintegration of the sensate form of Western culture and society, which emerged at the end of the twelfth century and gradually replaced the declining ideational form of medieval culture. For the past four centuries it has been dominant. In the period of its ascendancy and climax it created the most magnificent cultural values in most of the compartments of Western culture.... However, no finite form, either ideational or sensate, is eternal. Sooner or later it is bound to exhaust its creative abilities. When this moment comes, it begins to disintegrate and decline.... Even if it does not mean the extinction of Western culture and society, it nevertheless signifies one of the greatest possible revolutions in our culture and social life (28).

The "sensate form" is essentially that of modern materialism and its associated Enlightenment structures. Long exhausted, sunk in the retrospective mood, recycling modernism, and so on, the decline is evident, heralding, unbeknownst to itself, at times, an epochal change of the greatest magnitude:

> As such, it is infinitely deeper and more significant than the partisans of the 'ordinary crisis' imagine. A change

from a monarchy to a republic or from capitalism to communism is utterly insignificant in comparison with the substitution of one fundamental form of culture and society for another—ideational for sensate, or vice versa. Such shifts are very rare phenomena. As we have seen, during the thirty centuries of Greco-Roman and Western history they occurred only four times. But when they do take place, they produce a fundamental and epoch-making revolution in human culture and society (29).

...when their creative forces are exhausted, and all their limited potentialities are realized, the respective culture and society either become petrified and uncreative (if they retain their already exhausted form) or else shift to a new form which opens new creative possibilities and new values. All the great cultures, indeed, that remained creative underwent just such shifts (25).

Such is the scope of the "shift" or change that Western and global civilization now requires, not some half-way fix and tinkering, but truly an overhaul of the entire collection of sensate and Enlightenment categories of thought. In the long run only such change can produce a way forward into the future that resolves the dilemmas of modernity while preserving the best out of the Enlightenment, indeed, fulfilling the best in the Enlightenment and carrying it to fruition, around the globe, in the Imagination, and in reality.

In the meantime, in "A 'Post-Secular' Society—What does it mean?" (2007), the German sociologist and philosopher Jürgen Habermas, in a lecture delivered at the Nexus Institute at Tilberg University, addressed much of what a global civilization must include to bring people together from all religious and secular points of view:

Were secular citizens to encounter their fellow citizens with the reservation that the latter, because of their religious mindset, are not to be taken seriously as modern contemporaries, they would revert to the level of a mere *modus vivendi*—and would thus relinquish the very basis of mutual recognition which is constitutive for shared citizenship. Secular citizens are expected not to exclude *a fortiori* that they may discover, even in religious utterances, semantic contents and covert personal intuitions that can be translated and introduced into a secular discourse. So, if all is to go well, both sides, each from its own viewpoint, must accept an interpretation of the relation between faith and knowledge that enables them to live together in a self-reflective manner.

Although Enlightenment categories of thought limit Habermas' thinking, his presuppositions typically those of the struggle between it and Christianity, a shortcoming so often found in academic discourse, not universality, he states, "the selfsame normative expectations that rule an inclusive society" are incumbent and "prohibit a secularistic devaluation of religion." Citizens in the multicultural societies of the West, by extension elsewhere, must participate in a "complementary learning process" that does not seek to purge any voice from the public space, while creating a "balance between shared citizenship and cultural difference." As demonstrated earlier by his terms "new age movements," "'California' syncretism," and "de-institutionalized form of religious observance," he doesn't ultimately understand what's involved, like many in secular circles, part of the problem. Yet modernity has long been working on these accommodations as some of the finest fruits of the Enlightenment to heal the cultural divide that has often wracked modern societies, as further steps toward universality.

In 1928, Julien Benda, the Frenchman and author of *The Betrayal of the Intellectuals*, was one of the earliest observers of the rise of modern nihilism and its pernicious influence on literature and culture. Leveling a particularly prescient critique of Nietzsche and Marx, Benda wrote that of such decadent men of letters, it was hard "to imagine them turning against the tide

117

of their intellectual decadence and ceasing to think that they display a lofty culture when they sneer at rational morality" (155). Even as early as 1928, Benda realized they were beyond the reach of rational argumentation, locked away in their loathing and intolerance of moral and spiritual categories of thought and would not tolerate any such perspective. Sunk deep into a state of intellectual, moral, and spiritual decadence, holding humanity in their death grip, many loathe even the very idea of morality and spirituality. Although Benda's understanding comes out of the lesser universalism of the Catholic Church, he is right when he states, "The nature of moral action is precisely that it creates its object by affirming it." Everywhere, around the globe, where nihilism has performed its paradoxically salutary function of clearing the ground, it yet suppresses the universal at precisely the time when humanity needs it the most, to save ourselves from self-destruction. Benda's vision, though, like that of Barzun, Milosz, Chaudhuri, Rieff, and Sorokin, the ancients, Plato, Ibn Khaldun, Vico, and Washington, is not ultimately a despairing one. All of them evoke the possibility and time when, as Benda writes, "a handful of men at desks" are "able to succeed," once again, in helping "humanity believe that the supreme values are the good things of the spirit." Now on our laptops, uploading to our blogs and global social networks.

The Post-Gutenberg Revolution
A Manifesto

City Lights Books, in San Francisco, once asked me for a mission statement. The mission of Earthrise Press is to reach directly the reader, American and international, with works of a global, world-embracing vision. Here's a very incomplete list of self-publishers. Linger on them and think about it:

James Fenimore Cooper, Mark Twain, Walt Whitman, William Blake, John Milton, Henry Adams, Ezra Pound, e. e. cummings, Edgar Allan Poe, James Joyce, D. H. Lawrence, Gertrude Stein, Anais Nin, Carl Sandburg, Stephen Crane, Laurence Sterne, Thomas Paine, William Wordsworth, Jane Austen, John Ruskin, George Bernard Shaw, Rudyard Kipling, Thomas Hardy, A.E. Housman, Oscar Wilde, Virginia Woolf, Benjamin Franklin, Henry David Thoreau, Michel de Montaigne, Friedrich Nietzsche, Johannes Kepler, Alexandre Dumas, Derek Walcott, Upton Sinclair, W. E. B. DuBois, Edwin Arlington Robinson, and Robert Hayden.

Now tell me publishers have any special ability to identify and recognize writers who are actually writing something new and worthwhile. Why should any writer be the least bit ashamed about self-publishing today? I reject the self-serving slurs of corporate publishers wielded against independent authors and publishers. Most of these independent authors rarely published other writers. I haven't and won't. What for, when they can publish themselves? My point isn't for writers to send me their manuscripts. It's for them to realize that they can publish and market their own books worldwide, directly to the reader, for a very nominal investment, mostly of time, by merely using the technologies that already exist. Doing that is only going to become easier.

The Internet and other digital, technological developments make independent publishing and distribution more of a possibility than ever for the serious poet and literary writer, weary of the small little postmodern theories of self, academia, Marxism, deconstruction, race, gender, and so on, *ad nauseam*. Endless regurgitation of all of that, and similar academic banality, the classroom tripe of the lecture hall, is not part of the mission.

The mission of Earthrise Press is to publish my work without giving away control of my writing and 88% of the list price to the corrupt corporate conglomerates, distributors, cliques and coteries, large and small, of which I'd include, in addition to the obvious New York and international corporations, university presses, and mega-chain bookstores, Small Press Distribution, CLMP, the American Academy of Arts and Letters, Academy of American Poets, the American Library Association (ALA) and the journals that it controls, as well as those like them, *Poets & Writers* (the entire MFA mentality that goes with it), and other gatekeeping organizations that attempt to filter, regulate, exploit, and manage independent writers, and the small and supposedly independent presses and magazines, which largely share a very common and predictable worldview.

I've studied and sacrificed for over forty years to write my books, and I urge other writers to think and act for themselves, and take control of their work. Poets have as much right to publish and market their own writing and make a living from hawking their wares as anyone else. Remember the ballad-mongers and poets selling their broadsides on the streets of London. There is no reason why poets and writers shouldn't sell their own books to the entire world over the Internet. The New York mega-publishers and others elsewhere are not arbiters of literary quality and taste but economic self-servers selecting and promoting a very narrow, predictable vision of life, usually suffused with nihilism, in our extremely, extremely fragmented culture, while calculatingly discrediting, with slurs of "self-publishing," as though it were vanity publishing, any author intelligent enough not to conform or allow themselves to be exploited by them. The *poète maudit* pose and the academic route amount to about the same thing. It's long past time for the poet and writer to have a new relationship to publishing and the reader.

As Jason Epstein has said regarding his Espresso Book Machine, we are living in the most significant revolution in publishing since Gutenberg. Philosophically, at the center of that revolution is the individual breaking free of the old orthodoxies, as a result of accelerating decentralization and democratization, in publishing, literature, and knowledge, as in other domains of the Global Age. I highly doubt that William Blake and many of the writers mentioned above would have hesitated to join the Post-Gutenberg Revolution. The challenge of the Post-Gutenberg Age for poets and writers is to realize that there isn't any reason why one shouldn't sell one's own books directly to the reader, that one can, and that in fact there is every reason why one should.

In 2009, Clay Shirky, regarded by many people as the Marshall McLuhan of the Internet Age, in "Newspapers and Thinking the Unthinkable," announced what had already become an undeniable fact:

> It makes increasingly less sense even to talk about a publishing industry, because the core problem publishing solves—the incredible difficulty, complexity, and expense of making something available to the public—has stopped being a problem.

Later, in 2012, he observed, in "Napster, Udacity, and the Academy," addressing the massive change taking place, what has long been the stance of much of the publishing industry and the academy:

> Once you see this pattern—a new story rearranging people's sense of the possible, with the incumbents the last

to know—you see it everywhere. First, the people running the old system don't notice the change. When they do, they assume it's minor. Then that it's a niche. Then a fad. And by the time they understand that the world has actually changed, they've squandered most of the time they had to adapt....

That is much of the story of the response to the Post-Gutenberg Revolution by American and British publishers. The Post-Gutenberg Age has passed the torch back to readers, who have always been the true arbiters of who and what is worth reading, often, now, discovered through social networks, as on Facebook, Google Plus, Twitter, and reviews on Amazon and Goodreads, and elsewhere, readers telling other readers, through the power of the traditional word of mouth gone digital.

I define "Post-Gutenberg" as those digital changes in the techne of the culture and publishing that open up the relationship between writers and readers to a wider level than ever before experienced in history, enabling a much more direct communication, without or with fewer interfering middlemen and encumbrances, and now usually permitting dialogue to flow in both directions.

Papyrus, cuneiform clay tablets, rice paper, palm leaves, tree bark, vellum, deer skin, decorative gilt leather, chiseled marble, copper plates, silk scrolls for fastidious delectation—and now the electrons of ebooks—all found, and will find, their role and level. One thing all these forms of reading demonstrate is that the nature and experience of reading has through the centuries assumed numerous physical shapes. Yet not everyone will want to make the transition, and not for every type of book. Literary and artistic, cultural works, especially, will continue to preserve and honor, at times, the exceptional qualities of heavy weight and exotic papers, leathers. Under all the Forms, Platonic, the experience of the Archetype, the Idea, if you will, prevails and will continue, in the mind of a human being.

Those who worry about the demise of the book should take heart from history. But why waste so many trees on manuals, pulp fiction, the required textbooks that the overburdened backs of school children lug around, often unread—and the ephemeral newspapers that more and more people read online?

Jacob Epstein, who it is worth recalling is the veteran publisher and entrepreneur who invented trade paperbacks, founded *The New York Review of Books*, and is the driving force behind the Espresso Book Machine, has also observed, "Ebooks make the Gutenberg system, which still characterizes the industry after 500 years, absolutely obsolete." Publishing has advanced even from Print on Demand (POD) to ebooks, or Stage II of the Post-Gutenberg Revolution, while his EBM quite possibly might represent Stage III:

> E-publishing radically decentralizes the marketplace.... You're talking about every book ever written being stored at virtually no cost and delivered instantly on demand. Stores and even publishers are going to have to reinvent themselves.

His EBM already includes the entire catalogue of Ingram Book Company's Lightning Source and much of Google Books, seriously raising the possibility of every book in print, or ever published, estimated by some at 120 million books. The Revolution has incvitably led to many having realized, as J.K. Rowling has, that authors can "set up their own websites and eliminate the middlemen."

For years I've been occasionally reading Stevan Harnad's articles on the Internet about "Open Access," the archiving of peer-reviewed, scientific scholarly writing online for free access by other academics and researchers, starting with his "Post-Gutenberg Galaxy" of 1991. While I found his ideas compelling, he repeatedly stated that his thinking wasn't applicable to other types of writing but only that which is published in refereed scholarly journals, not written for trade, but for impact as shared research with colleagues. I tended to accept his conclusion, though wondered if it might not apply somehow to poets and literary writers, literature more broadly. When a new article by him would appear through a Google search or Google alert for "Post-Gutenberg," I would read or skim it, finding it interesting, but think there's not much I can do with him. Even he said so.

Then I read in 2010 a piece by Lawrence Lessig, a lawyer extensively involved in Internet issues, in *The Huffington Post*, "An Obvious Distinction," arguing "'open-source' is a practice that rests explicitly upon a respect for copyright." That's what I needed to hear. "The free choice of copyright owners to waive some portion of their copyright is not a rejection of copyright." It helped me realize that that is exactly what I and other writers had been doing for years and a missing piece of the puzzle in my own struggle for understanding the new dynamics of publishing, Post-Gutenberg and otherwise. I've "archived" a selection of my poems and essays on my website since 1998 and on my blog from the start in 2008. I view my hardcover and paperback POD books and ebooks as part of the same drive to reach a worldwide readership, conveying the fullness of what W. B. Yeats called *A Vision* only through my books. In other words, people can evaluate my writing in Open Access and decide if they're interested enough in my work to buy my books. Ebooks and POD make the distribution global and at a fair price by cutting significantly the traditional overhead of the middlemen, publishers, printers, distributors, and brick and mortar bookstores, allowing the literary writer to have the chance of actually making a living from his or her writing.

Shortly after reading Lessig, I noticed an article by Alan Rusbridger, a reporter in the UK, "The Splintering of the Fourth Estate." Rusbridger notes that "the mass ability to communicate with each other, without having to go through a traditional intermediary—is truly transformative." He cites the notion that traditional news publishing was "transmission," while the social networking of Web 2.0 has enabled "communication" in both directions, from writer to reader, reader to writer, more "personal." While his focus is on newspapers moving online, much of what he says is also applicable to literary writers. The ability to "friend" people around the world and communicate with them, on a person to person level, without politics and all the divisive issues always in the way, is incredibly "transformative." It opens up new possibilities in human consciousness, for understanding and cooperation, toward peace and the resolution of our many problems, at a time when we all need desperately to move together up the evolutionary chain of the species.

I especially appreciate Rusbridger's mention of Stowe Boyd, who comments on social networking in the following paragraph:

> I think that the rise of the social web, just like writing, the printing press, and the invention of money, is not really about the the end of what came before, but instead is the starting point for what comes next: richer and more complex societies. These technologies are a bridge we use to cross over into something new, not a wrecking ball tearing down the old.

Writers and readers alike, readers become writers, communication flowing both ways, we are all on an electronic ride across that bridge into the future, global as the network of human consciousness itself, as within the neural networks of the brain, evolving now on global social networks as never before, toward the transformation of the entire political and economic system that encircles the globe.

Far from bleak, the collapse of the corporate monopoly of publishing would be a tremendously promising development, already well advanced, with no escape for the publishing oligarches of New York and elsewhere. And it would bode well for a resurgence of intellectual energy and free speech, as well as a truly global market for the writers who master the necessary skills. "Scale" now belongs to the writer. That's the

Post-Gutenberg fact. The entire culture would be much better off with a true marketplace of ideas flourishing and competing for the reader. I offer my EarthrisePress.Net website as a model of one writer's effort, groping forward.

The vast majority of discussion about Post-Gutenberg publishing has been apocalyptic in tone or has and is attempting to transfer the monopoly of the mega-publishers to the Internet. That's entirely wrong in my opinion. There's every reason to celebrate the Post-Gutenberg Revolution. I read once someone referring to "PR-driven celebrity authors. That's what I call vanity publishing." That's exactly what the mega-publishers have been doing for decades, increasingly with the celebrity schlock they fob off as worth the time of the reading public, for which such publishers have no respect and no sense of the duty and calling of the true nature of the publisher and writer, instead trivializing the culture. The mega-corporate publisher's propaganda basically deceives the public about its supposedly special ability to identify and promote the most worthwhile authors, in order to create and maintain a stranglehold on who receives a hearing in the public forum. That has long been a major cultural problem in addressing the dilemmas and conflicts of our time. The Post-Gutenberg Revolution is sweeping aside the mega-publishers for very good reasons, as well as the bookstores that choose to do their bidding.

Many people, even in literature and poetry circles, and the universities, don't know what to think of a book unless someone "authoritative" tells them. The broad, liberal humanism of modernity, the result of the expansion of education, was supposed to remedy that dilemma. The Myth of the Enlightenment has only created its own meta-myths that have become oppressive in their own turn, suffusing culture, including publishing, journalism, and the media, as well as other echelons of thought. The problem is perennial to human development, through antinomies, the deep tensions and struggles of the soul.

I believe more writers and poets will learn how to take control of their own writing, though many writers have been content to wait around for someone else to decide their fate. Amazon, Kobo, Apple iTunes, etc., are all attempting to create an alternative to the traditional publishing house but notice every one of them operates in the best interest of its own company, not necessarily readers, writers, and independent publishers. To be fair, 35/65 and 50/50 splits and more on the royalties are way beyond 12/88%. James Fenimore Cooper and Mark Twain, and others, amassed real fortunes through self-publishing. Their percentage of the royalties had to be closer to what the Digital Age makes possible.

Why do most writers accept the New York mega-publishers' self-serving propaganda? Why do so many readers? Someone else is doing the thinking. Reflect on literary and cultural history. "Authoritative"? How did church "authority" regard Voltaire, Bayle, and Diderot? What did the "authorities" think of Blake? The Calvinists of Emerson, Whitman, and Dickinson? Nietzsche? And so on, and so on. Literary history constitutes the story of one stultifying convention or vision of life, one after another, fancying itself otherwise. Our time is no different, wrapped up in the academic clichés of the Enlightenment and the Decline of Everything, preening and flattering itself as having the meta-narrative of Truth, while denying and concealing the claim.

The corporations that have largely taken over publishing during the last few decades, since the 1980s, conglomerating independent houses under their umbrellas, purging many outstanding editors, function in a highly similar fashion. In a sense, the gauntlet thrown down by writers before "authorities" remains perennially about the same, in terms of structural dynamics, while the majority of "readers" are, I can imagine a *poète maudit* saying, "cattle." The challenge is always before the readers whom Stendhal called the "lucky few." It's well known that writers have always promoted their own work, had to, more so even now. Czeslaw Milosz is a good example of that, more than many realize. The traditional publishers have long been bankrupt. It's the reader who counts. Real writers are willing to compete for readers by striving to write something worthy of them, the "general reader," whatever the genre or form may be, to serve them, at any cost, out of a sense of duty to the culture and civilization.

The digital, Post-Gutenberg Revolution essentially has evolved the tools for the independent writer to go "viral," as a result of the natural selection process of readers. It began years ago in the sub-genres. It seems to have been delayed so long in trade books that one might be justified in wondering about collusion or at least the stranglehold the media corporations have over reviewing and preventing change. Yet we've already entered a new age. Far from bemoaning it, I counsel charge forward. Don't let the nay-sayers deter you.

Why should writers worry about corporate publishers? Writers have been exploited by them for centuries. As a poet, I'm concerned with what's best for readers and writers and believe publishers have stopped serving the best interests of the culture. They're not even capable of it anymore. It's long been observed that corporate conglomerates do very little to promote a book, and over the decades have come to do less and less for the author, especially in some genres.

For the most part, the books that receive an advance have increasingly become the popular fiction and non-fiction and talking-head drivel, much of it ghost-written, that largely betrays and undermines the culture in favor of shareholders, doing little to nothing for real writers, literature, or the civilization, in fact, eroding it. In the Post-Gutenberg Age, most writers who are taking the deceptive carrot of an advance ought to think twice and do the math. The entire thrust of the digital revolution has been towards greater freedom and independence of the individual from oppressive control of one kind or another. As self-appointed gatekeepers, corporate publishing conglomerates merit only to be swept into the dustbin of history, following the descent of the music industry, film photography, print newspapers, and similar dinosaurs.

The Internet, POD, Jason Epstein's Espresso Book Machine, ebooks and other developments have already demonstrated during the last decade and more that marketing and distribution channels no longer reside solely with publishing conglomerates, who in all actuality ceased serving literary authors and books long ago, and have become an impediment to the advancement and preservation of a culture worth living in. The individual author no longer needs the traditional publishers. The writer's goal is emphatically no longer wanting someday to be "picked up" by a corporate publisher. The fact that is becoming increasingly apparent is that authors no longer want them. Around the globe, readers are already realizing that the best writers are increasingly not to be found on the publishing lists of the corporate monopolies, tipping the balance toward the future forever. It is happening much faster than many publishers realize, stuck in desperately trying to preserve and transfer their monopolies to the Internet, instead of seeking new Post-Gutenberg relationships with writers.

With time, writers are only going to come to the realization all the more, if they haven't already, that the technology now exists to market and sell their own books, both POD and ebooks, directly to the entire world through one's own website, and the aggregate and affiliate online booksellers. Again, for a very small monetary investment, any writer with moderate technical computer ability can go around all of the traditional publishers, marketing and selling to the entire world, not just the USA. The POD and the ebook markets are truly global. That's what's so fascinating. Facebook and other social networking make reaching that global market possible, to the extent that they are not distorted by the corporations that own them and government interference, as well as hackers harboring various malicious motivations.

Ebooks are about what's good for readers, and, I would add, what's good for writers. The publishing middlemen are the ones who have gotten in the way for centuries, manipulating who receives a hearing and who doesn't, essentially depriving readers of diverse voices and perspectives. Ebooks provide the means for writers to communicate directly with readers, making again the reader the real judge of what's worth reading, as they have always been, ultimately, and what's not, though it should always be remembered that every great book also judges its reader. Can they understand it?

I believe ebooks will continue to take over a significant portion of the market-share of traditional publishing, possibly surpassing POD, while the Espresso Book Machine evolves, all of which will grow and serve their segments of the book market. Ebooks solve all the printing and distribution problems of publishing. Most importantly, ebooks solve all the problems confronting the writer and the reader. I'm not interested in solving problems for the mega-corporate publishers; they are the problem. The sooner writers and readers can largely get rid of them, and their interference in who and what can potentially receive a hearing from readers, the better. It's the reader who should be judging who and what is worth reading. Not the corrupt gatekeepers. The Digital Age offers the individual reader an exciting challenge.

The traditional "authorities" in publishing and culture have all revealed themselves as hollow and discredited. Democracy and the expansion of the freedom and liberty of the individual wants to move to the next level, the globe. Communication, information and dialog, aesthetic and literary expression, all are pushing forward to the widest scope and vista of freedom, the Earth itself. The throbbing, digital Network has laid down the fiber-optic cable and the Wifi, along with the resources of Web 2.0, so that it can happen.

Many, though, continue to overestimate the value of traditional publishers and what publishing with them amounts to and underestimate how much change has already taken place and how little the traditional publishers of poetry and literature in the United States actually have to offer. Compared to independent publishing, there are no decent contracts with traditional publishers. Given that they're suffused with the clichés of the Enlightenment paradigm, a now largely classroom construction, they're not capable of recognizing or promoting anything really new and significant in literature. They're a large part of the reason that a very dead and decadent literary period continues to drag and linger along.

Banding together into a coterie has always been a sign in literary history of exhaustion, imaginative, spiritual, literary exhaustion. That's what much of the problem is with the art. Ebooks and ereading offer a way to go around the manipulation with which the art has been controlled for decades, often by publishers and self-appointed cliques. The Post-Gutenberg Revolution represents a tremendously exciting sign of hope. As the global *lingua franca,* English has already demonstrated an astounding vitality in other cultures, inspiring writers everywhere with the hope of reaching readers around the world among the more than 1.8 billion people who now speak English.

While not all writers have the ability nor desire to handle the technical issues involved with websites, html, ebook formats, marketing, and other such things, given the wide range of human ability, there will remain a place for many of the intermediaries (often predators) who have forever made a living off writers and self-publishers of various quality. They, too, have been making the transition to the Internet for more than a decade and a half, in all formats and many venues.

All of those technical issues are much easier than writers who feel intimidated by them realize. For instance, there are only about a dozen html codes one has to learn to transfer a manuscript into an ePub or Kindle book. Anyone who has already put a website together won't find it difficult. Most who can use a wordprocessor and html editor have the skills. Many computer programs exist for creating ebooks which by pass all of that. It has been observed that publishers would be mistaken if they allow themselves to think there are major technical hurdles that are going to save them.

As examples accumulate of writers who have put it all together, in addition to the prerequisite of being real writers, fewer and fewer writers will turn to the traditional publishers. They simply don't have anything to offer. They betrayed whatever credibility they ever had long ago. Jason Epstein's *Book Business* is only one notable work that muses on the deeper issues at the core of the problems of publishing. They're also intimately connected with all the problems of higher education and the cultural angst of Enlightenment modernity. Most of the current corporate publishers and mergers have only been around for a few decades and mark a definite decline, in their own way, for publishing and culture. For the most part, recovery and renewal lies not through them, but around them, despite them. In diminished forms, most of them will probably linger on for some time, but the writer is better served by a contract directly with Amazon, Kobo Books, Barnes & Noble, Lightning Source, and other quality vendors, and selling his or her books directly to readers, which will become ever-more commonly done. Many already consider it the only credible way now to publish.

The kind of general non-fiction and run-of-the-mill fiction that publishing has become for most of the culture are not an encouraging sign, nor are the books the new online book publishers and vendors are usually choosing to promote on the home page of their sites. Indeed, it bodes ill, demonstrating that the corporate mentality has no sense of the social obligations that publishing at its best was and should entail. They are not book people. They are not people concerned with culture. They really don't know what it is nor can they properly judge it. They're destroying it by being only out for the money. They're unwittingly standing, too, in the way of real change.

I'm more interested in reaching the audience that Saul Bellow was fond of reminding people actually existed, and which continues to exist, awaiting always the writers and books that will help it move to a higher level of consciousness, the roughly 50,000 to 100,000 and more, perhaps some millions, college educated, general readers in the USA and elsewhere interested in and capable of understanding serious cultural and literary issues, discussion, poetry and literature, as in the case of Allan Bloom's *The Closing of the American Mind: How Higher Education Has Failed Democracy and Impoverished the Souls of Today's Students*—global readers and issues now. I believe that kind of success can now be done without the New York publishing cartel, despite them, since they really stand with the conventional university mentality in opposing anything beyond their own limited and defective sense of what should be published, what's possible and "enlightened," actually now hackneyed, benighted, and commonplace, part of our cultural dilemmas, not seeking to open up new perspectives. For decades, many thoughtful students have left the university disgusted with its dehumanizing sophistries. They are readers who might recognize what's new.

Far from publishers having a "reason to be happy about how the book market is evolving," as Mike Shatzkin, a publishing consultant claimed in 2010, it demonstrates that neither he nor they really understand that the dynamics involved embrace the entire world culture, of which they are only one small part, guaranteeing that the day approaches when they, too, like the music oligarchs, will be swept aside with the fiber-optic speed of the up-loaded gigabytes of the Post-Gutenberg Revolution, all the more clear in 2014.

I have become increasingly interested in and absorbed by the philosophical and social implications of the Post-Gutenberg Age, not only in terms of publishing itself, but also at the much deeper level of the global implications, as we move forward. The drive of intellect, soul even I would say, is fullness of Being, into what that means for our transformative age, from the long perspective of history. Someone once asked for my "agenda." If I had an agenda, it would be something like the following:

Implementation of many of Robert Reich's recommendations in his book *Aftershock* (2010) and other writings, including or in addition to:

133

Reinstate the Glass-Steagall Act
Reverse Citizens United
Increase the Graduated Income Tax to 70 to 80% on the mega-wealthy and corporations
Tax and regulate the plutocrats into submission
Limit and regulate corporate lobbying
Revive and expand the public financing of elections
End the military-industrial-congressional alliance
Arrest and imprison perpetrators of corporate bribing of politicians through "campaign contributions"
Prosecute and imprison politicians who accept bribery
Require profit sharing of all corporate wealth above a determined level with its producers
Follow Thomas Jefferson's advice: rescind the 1913
   Federal Reserve Act and create a US national bank
that lends 2 to 1, instead of 20 to 1
Break up the mega-media monopolies into at least a hundred entities
Create a single-payer national health care system
Change the nature of health care to prevention
End all reliance on non-renewable resources
The Supreme Court must protect the people from the ultra-wealthy. If not, the other Branches of Government must confront the situation
Elect Senator Elizabeth Warren the next President of the United States of America in 2016
Develop the United Nations into a global
representative system of cooperation and governance

Ultimately, the cultural shift will produce and necessitate a practical, political one. The underdeveloped United Nations is its forerunner. Change the thinking of the culture, and the politicians will have no alternative but to follow the people, or be left behind. That is the deepest implication of the Post-Gutenberg Age, the further evolution of global consciousness, a global ethic and culture, finding form, ultimately, in a political union serving all humanity.

While I agree with those who say the roots of many of today's conflicts stem from the way in which borders were drawn up after WWI, which has become a truism, other, perhaps even more problems stem from the contemporary failure to remember the experience of WWI and WWII, the extreme suffering and horror of both conflicts that led leaders everywhere to seek refuge in international cooperative organizations. Too often leaders today cynically consider the United Nations as a "tool" of the nation-state, national policy, marginalizing and deriding it, if not with their words, their actions. Humanity is in danger of repeating the experience of former generations, to relearn the lesson—unfettered nationalism is an unmitigated curse upon the face of the Earth.

In terms of Clay Shirkey's "The Collapse of Complex Business Models" (2010), think not only of outdated nationalism but also of the New York mega-publishers, and those literary magazines, institutions, and academicians who have a stake in and promote the long-decaying, collapsing vision of Enlightenment clichés. Yet Clay Shirkey and others are wrong about needing new filters. The Post-Gutenberg Age is about getting rid of filters and gatekeepers, while demanding that the individual become more responsible in the exercise of his or her freedom, and thereby actually expanding the filter to the general reading public, the analog being the body politic. The democratization and decentralization of the Internet, and the Post-Gutenberg Age, are the greatest challenge to the old model of publishing. Hence, it's the opening up of access to knowledge and information, communication broadly, that's taking place. The Gutenberg means of production, if you will, aided the king and his minions to maintain a tight control over what received a hearing. While corporations, advertisers, and government entities are seeking and have found ways to reinstitute such control online, the individual spirit has found and continues to seek independent means to express itself and communicate through the new mediums, despite inevitable interference, and what Saul Bellow called "The Great Noise," now online.

The entrenched schools of thought are obsessed with controlling and manipulating what people can find available to read, as Philip Rieff so cogently understood. They share that impulse in common. That impulse runs very deep in human nature. I've always known that and recognized it as one of the fundamental problems for an independent writer and publisher to have to deal with, but the evolving Post-Gutenberg discussion has opened it up much more to view online—and the extent to which it is really still running counter to the entire direction of the Post-Gutenberg Age. Indeed, contrary even, in a sense, though some would deny it, to the entire modern democratic age or global revolution, which, for centuries, has been about expanding and protecting the liberty and freedom of the individual.

They're running scared. Their pitiful dirge, how do we remain in control? They believe they know and can identify what people should read. What's good for the little people. Hubris. Arrogance. The whole system of the major publishers, the academy, and librarians, scratching one another's back, is coming to an end, changed by the new forms of social networking made possible by the Internet. Generations of exploited writers are exulting in their graves.

To the extent that the mega-portals and other venues are attempts to corner the ebook market through their online stores, I believe the merchants that will recognize, allow, and defend individual freedom of choice will win out in the long run. The leading ebook formats now open the way for the majority of books to reach the global marketplace and reader. All the software and requisite tools and venues are in place for the Post-Gutenberg Revolution to burst fully onto the world stage, with ultimately most books being published as ebooks.

The trash that has always come out of the major publishers is appalling. During the last twenty years or more, publishing has failed literature and culture in every conceivable way, for all the well-known reasons I have already cited and discussed. Suffice it to say that derision of self-publishing flies in the face of literary history. Almost every literary writer worth reading had to publish their own work in order to receive a hearing. Writers should vehemently reject the self-serving deceit and contumely that the major publishers use to exploit and steal from them the profit of their own labor. "The butcher, the baker, the candlestick maker," all have the God-given right to make, market, and sell the fruit of their labor, and writers and poets are no different. Jump out of the "rotten potato" of the nursery rhyme and corporate publishing. We have every right to make, produce, and sell our own books for the financial benefit of ourselves and our own families, and any and every assertion to the contrary is a contemptible lie. As the poet and independent publisher Robert Hayden wrote, he was not a character out of *La Bohème*. Writers who cherish that cliché may go ahead and give 88% to corporate philistines and exploiters. I, for one, prefer to follow the example of William Blake, other independent writers and poets, who had a measure of self-respect and initiative, with a brain in their head, some of whom amassed significant fortunes from their own sweat, toil, and sacrifice, instead of handing it over to contemptibly illiterate corporate conglomerates and their venal board members and stockholders.

Having edited Robert Hayden's *Collected Prose* and *Collected Poems,* respectively in 1984 and 1985, I had cause to confront many of the issues that develop with copyright holdings under the Gutenberg regime. Many difficulties arise for a poet and his estate that need not happen under Post-Gutenberg publishing. Like most writers Robert Hayden's prose was scattered all over the publishing landscape, with copyright not reverting to him. The fees required to reprint his *Collected Prose* were comparatively exorbitant and resulted in not even recouping the costs of editing the book. Editing it while I was living in Japan, the mailing and reproduction costs alone far exceeded the negligible advance and any eventual return. More than a decade and a half ago, I began to realize that Post-Gutenberg publishing resolves all of the practical problems that arose with the Hayden Estate, leading to how I chose to publish my own books. Unlike Tolstoy, the Post-Gutenberg Revolution has allowed me to become my own Vladimir Chertkov.

Given the history of publishers and reviewers throughout literary history, their endemic failure to recognize what is new and worthwhile, it's hard to understand why any thoughtful reader would look to them. I cannot emphasize enough that it's the discerning readers who should be deciding who is worth reading, not self-appointed publishers, librarians, and corrupt review magazines and journals like *Kirkus Review*, *Booklist*, *Library Journal*, *Publishers Weekly*, and other publications, servile and obeisant to the ruling ideologies, assumptions, and hackneyed tastes. Throughout the literary history of all nations, coteries have always developed, and they always seek to maintain their vision of life long past its day, as is the case now with postmodernism and postmodernity, the dregs of the Enlightenment. The mediocre cluster in groups, journals, reviews, to prop up one another, as Samuel Johnson so perceptively understood and satirized in the pages of *The Idler* in the 18th Century. Similarly, the corrupt academy, with all its attendant strangleholds on literary and intellectual life, has enabled postmodernism to drag on for far too long, seeping into every level of modern society.

I'm for exploring the possibilities beyond the rigidities of the entrenched worldviews that limit the individual writer, keeping the entrenched alive, on life-support, as it were. I stopped looking to the major publishers for anything new in serious literary writing long ago and think many insightful people have. The status-quo publishers are not interested in creative, serious writing, poetry or fiction, but what will sell, as is well known, the crudest, most intellectually shallow works of non-fiction and other pablum. I argue that there is now a chance that writers might really get paid for their work by taking control of it, taking it back from the illiterate corporate conglomerates who have no respect for serious literary and intellectual work. What they define as such has become nauseating banality, clichéd-ridden tripe, recooked Enlightenment drivel. The fulfillment of the Enlightenment is the Post-Gutenberg Age.

Part of the problem of The Transformation is that online reviewing has yet to develop sufficient alternatives that are intellectually engaging and enriching, with all too many blogs and websites that do review books online tied to corporate publishing interests, but things are improving, as everything moves to the Internet, and the thrill of freedom awakens the oppressed and the gifted. The traditional venues of review have long been atrophied, entrenched, while human experience has continued to evolve, far beyond them, which the old rags have blithely ignored, trapped in the already-written. The "established" reviews and magazines, all in various ways, have failed to keep up, stuck in their ruts, political, religious, or whatever, narrow assumptions, seeking to repeat literary and cultural history, imagining otherwise. By contrast, of course, as I once read someone assert, just dumping any heap of words into a mixer does not equal literature worth reading.

I have at times wondered if reviews are really as important as traditionally conceived. Such social networking sites as Facebook might add an interesting new component to the online dynamic, a new way for serious writers, with a demanding vision, to find the reader at a similar level, though nothing can replace an extended piece of prose, on or off line, by an intelligent and thoughtful reviewer, a rarity in any medium. The problem is always that most reviewers are tied to the old paradigm, can't see beyond it, continue to think in its terms. Similarly, much of the academy spurned literature long ago for "theory" and other philosophical, academic, and literary deadends, replicating the past through MFA programs, which channel more of the already-written to the "established" publishers, serving the prevailing nihilism.

Corporate publishers have been working diligently at corrupting the entire publishing industry for decades, in both the USA and the UK. It hasn't just happened overnight. It's taken a lot of bribe money in the deceptive form of "advertising," many hundreds of millions worth, not to mention the ceaseless takeovers of publishing houses that used to have decent editors in them who weren't just hacks for MBAs. As publishing was taken over and consolidated into the now five mega-media corporations, run by illiterate MBAs and other cultural ignoramuses, working for the 1%, looking for and thinking only of the "filthy lucre" on the bottom line, the level of literary ability and vision has steadily gone down, increasingly vitiating not only Western Civilization, but World Civilization, as its nihilism has been passed around the globe. The worthless "literary prizes" with which they try to prop up the crude and banal works they foist off as "literature" only proves how utterly corrupt publishing has become and are in themselves a means by which they seek to remain in control as arbiters. They no longer know what literature or civilization is and means, while arrogantly believing that they alone should be allowed to decide who and what receives a hearing with the people, with readers.

Fortunately, the Post-Gutenberg Revolution now provides a way to find and chart a new direction around the world and the tools with which serious writers of literary fiction and poetry can now bury the corrupt barbarians of the boardrooms who cynically dominate the media-scape, the black-ballers and manipulators of the literary market, propped up by media tycoons who have conglomerated the newspapers, radio, and TV stations into their despicable empires, robbing people of free and open debate, freedom of thought and information. We are at the end of a decadent and corrupt stage of civilization. To the extent that the decline of publishing has played a role in that process, much of it must needs be swept aside if we are to regain our balance and find the solutions to the vast problems that confront humanity. If the corporate publishers are going to continue to do business as usual, then the country and the world are better off without them.

The Quantum Physics of the Soul

"The first gulp from the glass of natural sciences will turn you into an atheist, but at the bottom of the glass, God is waiting for you." —Werner Heisenberg. 1932 Nobel Prize in Physics

"All of us living beings belong together in as much as we are all in reality sides or aspects of one single being, which may perhaps in western terminology be called God while in the Upanishads its name is Brahman." —Erwin Schrodinger, Nobel Prize for Physics, 1933; *My View of the World* (95)

"The general notions about human understanding... which are illustrated by discoveries in atomic physics are not in the nature of things wholly unfamiliar, wholly unheard of, or new. Even in our own culture they have a history, and in Buddhist and Hindu thought a more considerable and central place." —J. Robert Oppenheimer, *Science and the Common Understanding* (8-9)

As a young poet I read George B. Leonard's book *The Transformation: A Guide to the Inevitable Changes in Humankind*, in 1972, when it first came out. He was the vice-president of the Esalen Institute and one of the most articulate and far-sighted persons in the then-emerging human potential movement on the West Coast. It's not an exaggeration to say I devoured his book, reading and rereading it. Unfortunately, Leonard's book has perhaps somewhat fallen off the map, but it still speaks insightfully to the core problems of today, the need for a new sense of human consciousness on this planet. Following Leonard's citations, I branched into Alan Watts, Ram Dass, Carlos Castenada, Buckminster Fuller, Thomas Kuhn's *The Structure of Scientific Revolutions*, Quantum Mechanics, and ever more into Leonard's general openness to the East and to new conceptions of what is human, all of which I found myself still grappling with more than thirty-five years later, when I wrote my epic poem *The Parliament of Poets*. Leonard sums up *The Transformation* when he writes, "The time is overdue for the emergence of a new vision of human and social destiny and being." We have long been in the full flood of that time.

Similarly, Ervin Laszlo, long recognized as one of the most thoughtful and perceptive voices of the new consciousness movement, has written that many people are increasingly experiencing and awakening to a shift in consciousness, to "a subtle sense that we have lost touch with ourselves, and with the world" and that "we are in a race with time." "We either make it together, or we may not make it at all."

The traditional conception of religion, grounded in exclusivism, has become much of the problem, East and West, while the value of the way we actually live, mixed and poured together, especially in democratic pluralism, too often receives insufficient recognition by what purports to be "religion." Quantum Physics intimates a whole new way of understanding "religion" that can help heal the psychic wounds of modernity.

Part of our current problem, of our cultural moment, given the extreme degree to which we've become so fragmented, is that much of the culture, especially the academy, insufficiently understands its own claim of exclusive truth, its own meta-narrative, so locked in has the time become to various forms of exclusivism based in nihilism, if not atheism, that it is closed off to any type of spirituality, including even what Quantum Physics suggests, and so nihilism has not only Western civilization in a death grip but much of the world.

Broadly, much of the university, especially the humanities, to the extent that its vision of life entails nihilism, cynicism, endless formalisms, frivolity, the meaninglessness of life, which cannot be questioned, and is held in sacrosanct exclusive possession of the truth, usually justified with vague to perfunctory, knee-jerk allusions to the Enlightenment, as though that settled all of the profound human questions that people have asked throughout the ages for the rest of eternity, constitutes and represents the dehumanization of our time, i.e., both the traditional religions and nihilism are ironically sinking in the same boat. The ethos of the campus bureaucratic bean counter is nihilism.

Traditionally, "real religion" was always defined in terms of exclusivism, the challenge now is to realize that in a world of Quantum Physics "real religion," *ipso facto*, can only be defined in terms of universality, which is why the proponents of exclusivism who still cling to the old forms, whether "religion" or "secular," continue to lose ground, while the torch has passed to other hands, though often not informed to the same degree historically and culturally, which creates its own type of problematic fragmentation, yet seeking what's open, universal, beyond the old limitations that have created all the trouble in the first place.

The Greeks and other ancients wrote and recorded scientific discoveries in poetry because they believed it was the best language in which to convey the implications, often of unity and oneness, in terms of a universe composed of atoms, which is also partly my thinking behind writing *The Parliament of Poets*, because it is the best language with which to grapple with the implications of Quantum Physics, modern Monism. Similarly, I'd argue, the great Sufi poets realized there were things which can be said best only with the tongue of poetry.

The global confrontation with the mode of thinking in the old exclusive forms impels our Age to come to terms with resolving the negative baggage of modernity, of the Enlightenment, in a way that is both intellectually and spiritually satisfying and acceptable to people, broadly speaking, ideally, from all walks of life and points of view, traditional and secular, East and West. I believe Quantum Physics now makes that possible.

While not formulaic, I think it's the imaginative and artistic exploration of what the meaning and implications of Quantum might be, for human consciousness and otherwise, that can help us understand the problematic dimensions of the traditional claims to exclusivism, in a more universal, moderate, and scientific framework. Equally, the problematic dimensions of

143

science become Scientism needs to confront the spiritual implications of its own research in the fullness of the cultural perspective with which only the humanities and traditional religions can suffuse, enrich, and enliven it, with a new understanding of our common humanity, implicit in Quantum Physics, which can be brought to fruition and the attention of the general populace by the cooperative efforts of both humanists and scientists, understanding now the seriousness, necessity, and urgency of resolving the conflict between the "two cultures."

When young, I read Fritjof Capra's *The Tao of Physics* and *The Turning Point*. He has somewhat moved on from Quantum Physics to biology in his book *The Systems View of Life: A Unifying Vision*. Similarly, from elsewhere on the Olympian heights of science, rumblings can be heard of moving on, too, from Quantum Physics to other conceptions that perhaps a future epic poet will have to grapple with.

In *The Transformation,* George Leonard has a very choice quotation from the astronaut Neil Armstrong, from a dinner party conversation his daughter had had once with the first man to walk on the moon, looking back at Mother Earth, words I have remembered and reflected on for decades and try to honor in my epic:

"I want to tell you one thing. When I first looked back and saw the earth there in space, something happened to me." And then, in a lower more intense voice, "I'll never be the same."

Such experiences of "I'll never be the same" constitute the bedrock of what it means to be human, life after life, exploring it, widening the individual's consciousness and deepening the possibilities of our own self-understanding as a species on this planet, suggesting who we are and ways to save ourselves during this time of ongoing global crisis and transformation.

II Reviews and Interviews

Ben Jonson's *Bartholomew Fair*
2009

Having seen Antoni Cimolino's production of Ben Jonson's *Bartholomew Fair* a few weeks ago, at the Stratford Shakespeare Festival, in Canada, I find myself continuing to think about it. A rare play rarely played, Jonson's comedy, like Shakespeare's, offers its audience a serious vision of life in all its plenitude, letting the hot air out of everyone. Cimolino gives the play a marvelous interpretation, bringing it to life for our own time. After seeing the play, it was a shock to learn that the Stratford Festival production was the first performance in North America. *Bartholomew Fair* deserves to be much better known.

Bartholomew Fair was a yearly event in London, held from 1133 until 1855, when it finally came to an end. In Jonson's day, it attracted large crowds of people from all walks of life to its four days of commerce and carnival, in Smithfield, a less desirable part of London.

Rather than a synopsis, available elsewhere, what interests and fascinates me about *Bartholomew Fair* is its vision of resolution. The play is stocked with cut-purses, prostitutes, nitwits and fools, wooers and wooed, sanctimonious Puritans and scheming characters of all types. Judge Adam Overdo, a justice of the peace, dons a disguise and infiltrates the fair to spy for himself on the lower echelons of society that he deals with daily in court, to understand them better, and to note "enormities" for prosecution in many cases. Yet Jonson reveals Overdo to be as false and hollow as all the other characters, that is to say, human. From high to low, none are without flaw and failing, all are put under satire's cutting instrument. More than a morality play, the fullness and vitality of life are thoroughly explored and enjoyed, the delight of existence, all its antinomies opened to view, wisdom and delight. Tom Quarlous says to the Judge at the end, "Remember you are but Adam, flesh and blood! You have your frailty; forget your other name of Overdo and invite us all to supper." In an act of acceptance and humility, rather than benevolence, at the end of the day and play, Judge Overdo invites everyone to dinner at his own home, all passion spent.

A marvelous production. Juan Chioran's portrayal of the Puritan Zeal-of-the-Land Busy was brilliant. I would say one of the reasons the play probably fell into obscurity during the 17th century was Jonson's scathing satire of the Puritans. Even if the theatres had not been closed, it would have been too hot to handle under Cromwell and so forth. I hope Antoni Cimolino's revival of *Bartholomew Fair* leads to more appreciation and other productions. Perhaps our time is one that can enjoy and hear *Bartholomew Fair*. The play deserves to be high in the canon of 17th century drama and is a refreshing change of pace from Shakespeare, while sharing some of his best qualities, especially the Elizabethan resolution of all orders, an impressively humane and gracious ending, one worth pondering.

Lucy Peacock's Ursla the Pig-Woman, an enormously obese vendor of cooked pig, as well as a provider in her tent of other human wants, was outrageously funny at times, though a minor character. Having attended plays during most seasons at the Stratford Festival for the past decade, I couldn't help but recall her in other performances, which I much preferred, though I suppose it is the role Jonson wrote. A tremendous cast, Cliff Saunders performance of Lantern Leatherhead's puppet play of Hero and Leander was hysterically funny. He had me laughing almost to tears. A wonderful experience. A vision.

The American Scholar and the Decline of the English Department

Having read *The American Scholar* for probably over thirty years, I could feel only the most seething contempt for the Autumn 2009 article by William M. Chace, "The Decline of the English Department: How it happened and what could be done to reverse it."

I found myself repeatedly thinking while reading it, is this all you can come up with? What do you expect? The American English department is thoroughly sunk in doctrinaire nihilism and cynicism, as are all of the humanities, indeed, modern culture. We don't believe there's any value, meaning, or purpose to life. Who in their right mind would want to spend their lives studying the idiocies that the humanities have given themselves to over the last decades? I didn't in the 1980s when I found myself subjected to bumbling fools prating about Derrida and the End of Everything, while composition "specialists" were busy draining off, in their own way, anything worthwhile to write about. Clearly fewer and fewer young people are interested. Good for them. There's hope after all. Unfortunately, that leaves most of them grossly illiterate and nescient about human civilization. But that's what you ultimately get when you have coercion of conscience by tutors, clerks, and hacks, by Polonius spewing out his dehumanizing theories and abstractions.

William M. Chace does not ask a single, worthwhile question about why the decline of the humanities has taken place, but only gives the reader the usual academic platitudes, which I'm not even going to repeat, they're such a common coin, an old tale retold now for decades. How nauseating. The corrupt, coercive system deserves to decline, indeed collapse. Only then is there a small chance that people both inside and outside of the academy might begin to ask truly serious questions and seek truly serious answers. There's nothing serious about university studies today. With this article, *The American Scholar* has proven it for anyone in doubt.

The professionalization of literary studies has been disastrous. Who was it who said so many decades ago, in the 1920s or '30s, that the Ph.D. would destroy education? It definitely has. It's put ignoramuses, time-servers, and goose-steppers in the classroom in endless droves. Like produces like. Why is anyone surprised that they have burned down the Sacred Grove? They've destroyed literature, turning it into an academic plaything.

And who has assisted them? Worthless, illiterate university administrators, more interested in cynically maximizing profits, exploiting teaching assistants, professors, and everyone else on campus, sucking the juice out of state and federal funding. Having lost all sense of the duty to morally and spiritually cultivate students, administrators allow them to flounder along, happy to continue to raise costs and keep the money flowing in, often to themselves.

It's our whole vision of life that has become exhausted, not merely the English Department. William M. Chace's criticism of the fragmenting of the humanities into sub-disciplines obsessed with gender and ethnicity is an accurate assessment, but an old one by now. How do we recover what we have in common as human beings and humanists? You won't find an answer in *The American Scholar* or any other academic journal.

Similarly, all literary periods decline into coteries, with poets and writers attempting to shore up one another. In fact, it's part of human nature, to herd together, huddle for warmth, comfort, create a department. The weak, the untalented, and cowardly are especially given to this impulse. While it increases what passes with many for survival, those who go out of the cave in pursuit of the Real are the ones who slay the Beast, ultimately providing provender for the fearful and vulnerable. That is what all the great poets and writers did. Rabelais and Cervantes, Melville and Robert Frost, many others, into their heart and soul, not some university or creative writing program and the subsidies that keep their seemingly hegemonic dominance afloat. I first subscribed to *Poets & Writers* when it was the earliest incarnation of a newsletter in the 1970s. It was evident to me even then that a coterie was forming, analogous to so many, as with the Provencal poets, Japanese literature from time to time, and elsewhere. That it has become the sink hole or rapacious beast that it has is no surprise, known to all, who are discerning. I have thought for decades that there is only one way to slay it, the test and ordeal of the spirit that the greatest writers have always had to face and go through, that of writing the book that overturns the entire prevailing outlook, as Cervantes did with all the cloying works of chivalry. In other words, it must be earned through "perseverance" (Johnson on Shakespeare), diligence, independent study, confronting the darkness in one's own soul and time, and the blessings of the Muse.

Nothing could be more contrary to the cynical university system of patronage and extortion of public funds, by academic and poetry bureaucrats, which often passes for literature today. All the more reason that the lone, solitary writer, dedicated to the literary tradition of what is the most noble and true in human nature, seeking truth, not tenure, service, not the approval of parasites, can, as Saul Bellow phrased it once, "bury them," and reorient aright "the great ship of literature."

My advice? This world needs a new global vision of life on this planet. If English departments aren't capable of understanding, recognizing, and respecting that, what good are they? Are they even remotely capable any more of understanding what civilization is and supporting it? Maybe it's long past time for writers who have any self-respect to consider more carefully whether it's wise or not, for the culture, not merely themselves, to be associated in any way whatsoever with what the American English department has become. Throughout the history of English and American literature, most poets and writers had or wanted nothing to do with tutors. Again, Shakespeare's Polonius tells the tale. The migration into the academy really only began in the 1940s and '50s. Literature and poetry are not "play things," curios for discourse, but, as Robert Frost wrote, "play for mortal stakes." If scholars can no longer understand that, they don't merit the title. They do not own the Tradition, for all stand before it and are judged. If need be, closing down such English departments and Ph.D. programs, especially the "theory shops" and "institutes," corrupting organizations like the Modern Language Association (MLA), all Master of Fine Arts (MFA) programs, "studies" departments cannibalizing both intellectual life and what humanity has in common, would not constitute any loss to the great ship of literature, nor the culture. Once that's done, literature might stand more of a chance of recovering a noble, inspiring vision of the human being and deserving again the respect of the general populace. If that's beyond conception, read Tolstoy's *What is Art?* He may have been under the strain of fighting the drift of early modernity, made many errors, but at least he went down in battle, and is much healthier than many of the academic types one finds in American English departments, which have largely become a sacerdotal cult of nihilism, a priesthood indoctrinating their students into Nothing, preventing any serious challenge and debate from taking place, while prattling about free speech and conscience, namely, only theirs. Academicians themselves have declined, while whining about anti-intellectualism and philistines whenever they're met with real criticism, instead of sycophantic students desperately working on their Ph.Ds, though that seldom happens since they keep themselves so isolated.

William M. Chace's closing comments are feeble, if not pathetic. Aesthetics? We've been there for centuries. All recipes for further decline, accommodation, etc. Let's not feel bad. Let's put on a happy face. Sad but revealing of how bankrupt educated discussion has become.

Here's a novel suggestion not tried or seriously considered in most academic departments for some time now. In your office, get down on your knees and beg God to forgive you for what you've done to literature and the culture during the last forty years. We need to love God, to pray, and to seek out his will for humankind, in our day and time. Not as an academic "idea" or theory, but as a reality in our inmost heart and soul. We need to return to life the serious purpose that only a religious, spiritual vision provides, though pedants think it's their *raison d'etre* to strip young adults of it should they present upon entry into college. This change of heart is needed not merely in the university, but rather throughout modern, Western civilization, indeed East and West. I am arguing not for a simplistic return to Christianity or any one of the great religions, but to what lies universally at the core of all of them—the Divine Being beyond the ability of the human intellect to fully understand, but within our ability to experience through prayer, worship, and meditation. Then, literature might again offer a vision worth studying.

Fang Lizhi and Human Rights in China
2000

Since the Tiananmen Square massacre of 1989, Fang Lizhi has often been regarded as the foremost advocate of human rights in China. As one might well imagine, his championing of democracy and human rights has a long history going back as far as thirty years before Tiananmen Square. In 1957 he argued political ideology had nothing to contribute to scientific inquiry, which initially led the Chinese government to identify him as someone in need of correction. From time to time, several other clashes with the government took place. In 1986 the communist authorities believed he helped start the pro-democracy student demonstrations of that year. In 1987 he was dismissed as vice-president of the University of Science and Technology in Anhui province and thrown out of the Communist Party. His dismissal was clearly in retaliation for his fearless pro-democracy speeches throughout China and statements in the foreign press.

Although he did not participate in the Tiananmen Square demonstrations of 1989, the government accused him of counterrevolutionary activities and of instigating the demonstrations. When the bloody crackdown began, he realized his life was in danger and fled with his wife to the US embassy in Beijing. Forced to live in the embassy for an entire year before being allowed to leave China, he wrote four scientific papers and a number of acceptance speeches for the international awards that he increasingly began receiving in recognition of his heroic defense of democracy and human rights. Since his release, he has taught at Oxford, Princeton, and the University of Arizona, where he is now a tenured professor.

Before turning to his ideas on democracy and human rights, I believe it is important to understand why Albert Einstein is a significant influence on Fang Lizhi. As a prominent fellow scientist, one might well imagine Fang Lizhi to respect and appreciate Einstein's scientific achievements. More surprisingly though, he finds in Einstein's progressive social and political ideals an example of a public role for the scientist that he clearly thinks inspiring and worthy of emulation. Einstein of course had the experience of fleeing the Nazis and was always very politically involved in the struggle for a just social order. Especially during the last decade before Einstein died in 1955, he was an active spokesman for human rights and the United Nations, which he felt the Member States had nevertheless failed properly to design and support.

Fang Lizhi, then, conceives of himself, and must be seen properly in the light of, a universal struggle for human freedom and peace. In his 1992 book *Bringing Down the Great Wall: Writings on Science, Culture, and Democracy in China*, he often quotes Einstein not only on scientific matters but also on social and political ones as well. I quote only one reference in support of this fact: "Einstein's concept of world citizenship was profound. . . . in the years ahead, the human race will have to come to grips with this idea as well" (249).

Let's come to grips now with Fang Lizhi's statements on China. He himself has criticized the tendency in China and the West to conceive of China "as totally different from any other civilization in the world" and that therefore "universal principles of human rights don't fit China's experience" (*New Perspectives Quarterly*, Winter 1992). Far from unique despite its huge population, he insists "the Chinese people want the same freedoms as everyone else." Instead of accepting and even defending what he calls a "double standard" when it comes to China, Fang emphasizes the world community should "uphold human rights as a universal standard." The suppression of Falun Gong and other dissidents continues to cry out to the world for justice.

The exemplary quality of Fang Lizhi's appeal to the world community can be discerned in the following excerpt from "Patriotism and Global Citizenship," originally an interview taped in Beijing in February of 1989 just before the spring turmoil leading up to the Tiananmen Square massacre:

Human rights are not the property of a particular race or nationality. . . . These are fundamental freedoms, and everyone on the face of the earth should have them, regardless of what country he or she lives in. I think humanity is slowly coming to recognize this. Such ideas are fairly recent in human history; in Lincoln's time, only a century past, it was just being acknowledged in the United States that blacks and whites should enjoy the same rights. In China we are only now confronting such an issue. (247)

Here is the voice of a Chinese intellectual we ought to remember the next time the excuse of 1.2 billion people surfaces. Here is a voice of universal human importance reminding us of our own history and responsibilities and what we ourselves at times forget in exchange for business with China. On a number of occasions, Fang Lizhi has criticized the West and particular leaders for believing that trade with China is more important than human rights. With a striking clarity of moral vision, fearing for the long-term stability of Asia, he has pointed out that fascist Germany and Japan both had productive economies that far from resulting in liberal democracy ended in widespread regional and global destruction and misery for millions of people.

Having just read Fang's writings before leaving for China as a Fulbright-Hays scholar in early June of 1994, I sat in a lecture room of Beijing University with his words and ideas resonating at times in my mind. The lecturers represented a variety of points of view on Chinese history and culture. Those who were obviously presenting the party line scared or appalled me with their distortions of modern Chinese history and their defense of the abuse of human rights on a scale that is almost unbelievable. For those few who managed to find the humanity to affirm the truth about China's century-long tragedy of violence and chaos, no matter in how careful and guarded of a way, I felt the deepest respect. Here were voices of heroism, reminiscent of the noblest

Confucian scholarly traditions, who had the courage to speak the truth in a country in which many were still too afraid, and for good reason. One of my lasting impressions of China is that many individuals were palpably afraid to speak freely about issues of social, political, or public importance.

I was truly shocked and deeply moved by the revelation that the lecture room in which I and thirteen other Fulbright-Hays scholars sat every day for two weeks was used as a prison cell for twenty Beijing University professors during the first two years of the Cultural Revolution. Three times a day, they were forced to bow down to Mao's picture. Even more shocking and disturbing was to hear words, in the very same room, from some of my American colleagues, shamelessly supporting the Chinese communist revolution, as though China would be the country finally to get communism right. The Chinese setting highlighted for me the betrayal of democracy, at tax payer's expense, among some of my own nation's elite in an overwhelmingly devastating way. How could the words of Fang Lizhi not resonate in my mind?

We need soberly to remember the violence and oppression when we study or trade with China and remember that the moral, religious, philosophical crisis of China is fundamentally the modern one East and West share.

Bitter Winds, Indeed
2000

Returning in 1994 from China as a Fulbright-Hays scholar, I could not shake China off. It has become part of my consciousness forever. After writing an essay on classical and modern Chinese literature, with Confucius, Tu Fu, Lu Xun, Lu Wenfu, and other classical and modern writers fresh in my mind, I reread the writings of Fang Lizhi and continued to struggle to understand my experience in China. Appalled by the injustices of a political system that could imprison and destroy so many members of its own culture, from all walks of life, I then read in November of 1994 *Harry Wu's Bitter Winds: A Memoir of My Years in China's Gulag*.

Arrested in 1960 for reasons no real judicial system in the world would recognize, Harry Wu spent the next nineteen years of his life in one brutally subhuman labor camp after another until he was released in 1979 and eventually given permission to leave China for the United States. The victim of slave labor, starvation, and torture, Wu, at times broken physically and near death, endured with the hope of some day telling the world of his experience:

> My travels in 1991, when I returned to China to film [secretly] the conditions within the labor camps, fulfilled part of a consuming mission. Even though I had found safety in the United States, I had never found rest. Always I recalled the faces I had left behind. Always I worried that while I had escaped, the labor-reform system continued to operate, day by day, year by year, largely unnoticed, unchallenged, and therefore unchanged. I felt urgently the responsibility not just to disclose but to publicize the truth about the Communist Party's mechanisms of control, whatever the risk to me, whatever the discomfort of telling my story. Each time I revisited my past, I hoped it would be the last time, but I had decided that my experiences

belonged not only to me and not only to China's history. They belonged to humanity. (285-286)

Like so many accounts of the Soviet gulag, Harry Wu's is a voice of witness, of moral memory, compelled from within to speak the truth in the hope of finding justice before the universal court of humankind. Without relating the many tragic incidents of Wu's book, let me just say his words sank into me and left me deeply shaken, struggling further to understand the country I had just visited, struggling further to understand what the African-American writer Ralph Ellison was fond of calling "human complexity." Fang Lizhi's own words on Harry Wu's 1994 book are worth quoting: "The injustices he chronicles are still going on today. His special point of view on history and politics makes it possible to understand why a democratic China is a dream that shall never die." I was once more deeply distressed when Harry Wu was arrested in June of 1995, while entering China as an American citizen and on an American passport. His ordeal confirmed for me the side of Chinese political reality that I had painfully sensed and observed while there, and which all so unfortunately still continues as attested by the suppression of the Falun Gong and others.

It was while visiting Shenzhen, the city of the new economic policy, that I noticed the assistant to the mayor pick up from the meeting room table a copy of a speech he proceeded to read to our Fulbright-Hays group. Well worn, soiled, with the pages curling from repeated reading to one collection of foreigners after another, the paper described in glowing terms the achievements of Shenzhen's economic miracle. After handling us in apparently the usual way, when someone perceptively asked what the residency status of the three million workers in Shenzhen was, the mayor's assistant tried to put a good face on the fact that two million were on temporary internal work papers, primarily male, since a proportionate number of women and children are excluded from the "city," and subject to dismissal at any time back to the countryside. Looking out the bus window as we drove to the train station to Hong Kong, I could not but think of the Soviet Union's Potemkin villages.

Harry Wu's 1995 experience further confirms that such injustices as he chronicles are continuing today. In 1994 one of the unexpected sights I saw with my own eyes, by chance, in crowded Beijing traffic, was a man handcuffed and blindfolded, sitting in the back of a jeep, between two policemen, on his way somewhere he could not see. A few days later a Chinese friend who grew up in Beijing told me that only political prisoners are ever blindfolded. Far from China needing business now, and human rights later, China needs, as all countries need, human rights and democracy first and foremost and forever.

I remember reading that Eleanor Roosevelt, as chairwoman, served in 1947 on the Human Rights Commission with China's representative, Dr. Peng-Chun Chang, as vice-chairman. Together, along with members of eighteen other nations, they helped draft the Universal Declaration of Human Rights. According to her own testimony, Dr. Chang repeatedly challenged the Western representatives, reminded them of the importance of the ideas of Confucius on human rights, and argued philosophically for their incorporation along side those of Thomas Aquinas and other Western thinkers. It is historically accurate to say the resulting document is truly representative of the best of China's own philosophical thinking on human rights, basic human values.

I do not know whether Fang Lizhi or Harry Wu is aware of the contribution of China to the Universal Declaration of Human Rights. I do know I believe the following words by Fang Lizhi articulate the most profound vision of human life and experience now available to the consciousness of late twentieth-century human beings, East or West, a vision toward which we all must continue struggling to evolve:

The values that underlie human dignity are common to all

160

peoples. They are the universal standards of human rights that apply without regard to race, nationality, language, or creed. Symbolized by the United Nations' Universal Declaration of Human Rights, these principles are increasingly accepted and respected throughout the world. ("Keeping the Faith" 262).

Global Tragedies of Our Own Making
2000

I've often thought or returned to passages in Boutros Boutros-Ghali's *UNvanquished*: *A U. S. - U. N. Saga* since reading it in the early summer of 1999. Throughout the debate and defeat of the Comprehensive Test Ban Treaty (CTBT), the charades over Congressional withholding of funding to the UN, Jesse Helms' appalling performance before Security Council Members in January of 2000, my attending the Millennium Forum as an accredited participant at the UN in May 2000, watching and hoping the requisite will might be found at the Millennium Summit in September 2000, I have repeatedly found myself recalling Boutros-Ghali's devastating critique of US undermining of the United Nations, struggled to fight off a pervasive sense of tragedy and lost opportunity, lost since 1992 when Boutros-Ghali's *Agenda for Peace* was shunted aside.

How many echos I've heard from the couple of hundred books I've read on the League of Nations and United Nations. How frightening it has been to watch my fellow citizens so obsessed with their own little private, selfish worlds, turning away from international responsibilities and duties, scape-goating the UN for our own failures and loss of nerve. During the last year, I've been interviewed on over 230 radio stations about my own book, *Into the Ruins*, partly on the UN, in literary terms, and have heard firsthand all the extremist arguments against the participation of my country in the Organization, attempting to refute them as best I could.

There are many who understand the seriousness of the situation. William H. Luers, the President of the UNA-USA, writes a comprehensive appeal for UN support in his "Choosing Engagement: Uniting the U.N. with U.S. Interests" in the September/October 2000 issue of *Foreign Affairs*. The UNA, World Federalist Association, and others have done much to educate and elevate discussion about the necessity of our global

162

cooperation through the United Nations. Alas, I often doubt, in the end, such efforts will save the day. Boutros Boutros-Ghali's *UNvanquished* reveals why. Having read all the writings and memoirs of the UN Secretary Generals, I believe *UNvanquished* stands alone as the most insightful, courageous, heroic work ever written about the realities of the United Nations and its Member States, especially the US.

We cannot shunt aside the experience of Woodrow Wilson and FDR and expect to thrive. Having failed the League of Nations and themselves, the global community rose from the ashes of World War II to form a more perfect union. As the Millennium Summit has recently demonstrated on paper, while most of the US media ignored it, the Member States understand much of what needs to be done. Yet events already suggest they, we, still lack the will and shall quite likely have to suffer the dread forces of history in order to recover it.

To My Opposite Number in Texas
2010

Daniel Rifenburgh studied with Donald Justice and Richard Wilbur, with the latter providing an Introduction to Rifenburg's only book of poems, *Advent* (2002). Though not mentioned on the book flaps or in Wilbur's introduction, Rifenburgh, whom I've come to know through Facebook, was, he tells me, a student of the poet Robert Hayden, when he was a visiting professor of poetry at the University of Louisville during the spring semester of 1969. Since I myself had been a student of Hayden's at the University of Michigan a decade later, I was delighted to communicate with someone else who had also studied with him. We exchanged a number of messages. I ordered a copy of *Advent* and he mentioned he had ordered a copy of my book, *The Grove of the Eumenides*, which includes my essay "Robert Hayden in the Morning Time." He remarked "Hayden got me a creative writing scholarship," but he had never bought his *Collected Poems*, which seemed odd to me. If I had studied with anyone of Hayden's ability, though I don't know who that would have been, I would have at least read all his work and chosen to own his books. It's a pity that Rifenburgh didn't. He might have found much that would have helped in both form and content.

Though I have never cared for most of the poetry of either Richard Wilbur or Donald Justice, finding them small academic poets, campus poets, writing usually on narrow, personal, limited subjects, I thought I'd not hold that against Daniel Rifenburgh and tried to give an impartial reading to his poems, when *Advent* arrived. The Note on the Author informed me that Rifenburgh had spent three years in Vietnam after his study at the University of Louisville, which made me recall Hayden's bemoaning in poignant poems and prose his students "brutalized" in that conflict, wondering if he might have had Rifenburgh in mind among them. Wilbur's introduction didn't impress me at all, nor did his citing some lines from Rifenburgh, which included, "Wandering between the Word and its infinite extension." I can respect a poet who believes in Jesus Christ and whatever historically evolved denomination or persuasion he or she chooses, or dissents from. I am not entirely unsympathetic at all. I stem from a long line of Christians of many denominations. Christianity is a humane, spiritual, and true vision of life, when not corrupted by human beings, which is the problem, since we seem to have the capacity to vitiate everything we touch. I even find Christianity infinitely preferable to Marxism, capitalism as a religion, and the other endless substitutes for transcendence that modernity has and does produce. I'm well aware that by saying all of that I've violated numerous sacred doctrines, religious and secular, but must be honest before my own conscience, and what I actually found and think about Rifenburgh's poems.

Getting past the first poem was the problem. I can't even take it seriously in terms of what it's saying. "To My Opposite Number in Samarkand" is in epistolary form, addressed to someone in the East, who hears, "The gong inside the old Buddhist temple," and the call to prayer from "The high towers of the mosques." Nearby, the reader is told, stands "the lone orthodox church, unevangelistic." One senses there's a severe judgment in the word "unevangelistic," less than full sympathy with Eastern Christianity. Rifenburgh, I should explain, lives in Texas, perhaps known more for evangelism than the high church style, and maybe that influences his word choice. After allusions to Dante, Virgil, and Parmenides, the persona seems to take refuge in poetry, which is a thoroughly modern gesture, time honored for over a hundred and fifty years. What poet can quibble with that? Yet, an ersatz, nonetheless, and even Matthew Arnold knew and understood it as such. To his credit, so does Rifenburgh. He soon turns to the lines quoted by Richard Wilbur, after remarking on the overwhelming experience of reading Montale,

Or, so it seems, in the afterglow of such reading,
As if light had an enduring stepchild in the world
Wandering between the Word and its infinite extension,
Finding play in the interstices and lacunae
Where even breath must pause
In its tally of declensions
And what enters then by a grace
Commands our strictest reverence.

His "strictest reverence," for the Word, is further implied in the closing stanza, in which he writes to his "Opposite Number," to speak in the ear of the Bodhisattvas, by implication all the Ways of Opinion, "Parmenides." The subordinate clause, "if you're able," slips in a derisive note, sticking the interlocutor right in the guts, if he hasn't gotten it by now. In another poem, Herman Melville receives similar treatment, which I think constitutes a misunderstanding of Melville's complexity: "call it a lack," "a bible would do him little good."

"To My Opposite Number in Samarkand" and the last one in the book are clearly intended as "bookends," if you will, that frame the poems in between of mostly much broader range, with many on Rifenburgh's experiences in Texas and South America. His sequence of poems titled "Andean Music," for instance, explores his time working as a newspaper reporter in Latin America and Peru. I was struck in particular with the poem "VI. El Condorito," about "Che Ernesto," not the Marxist hero, but a local person known for flying down from the mountains of Machu Picchu in a hang-glider. Later, together, they "headed, in the dark before the dawn, up to the sacred city." Such poems are the best of his work, involved with life. In terms of other poems, Aristotle in his *Poetics* emphasized one of the crucial abilities of the poet was to choose the right material to work with. Rifenburgh often seems to me to lack such a sense of decorum, though our times may tend not to like that old tag. It is something poets forget and neglect at their peril. And it is always a temptation for the poet to write with his or her doctrine in mind and not the heart.

The last poem of the book is the title poem, "Advent," and the reader is meant to feel the weight of the book leading up to it, emphasizing its importance to Rifenburgh. After describing a rainy day and the material decay of various leaves, he writes,

The mind, too, sheds a tattered cloak

And recalls elements of the old story:
The hoop round the omphalos of Christ, Marian,
The cold coin imprisoning Caesar,
A tocsin of alarm dilating the pupils of Herod,
And now the heart shunts the oil
Of incarnation out of its chambers again
In time with the last drumbeats of the rain.
We defeat the world through surrogates, and but   briefly,
While placid beasts feed in drizzling pastures,
Building strength for the flight into Egypt,
Yet the son must be born in us, says the Father,
Or wither, when new oil floods the ventricles
And we become, however briefly, His surrogates
Or betrayers.
And for this, in Winter's dead zero,
We must sing, sing Hallelujah.

The choice laid before the reader is the exclusivism of truth, for, from whatever perspective, this truth is the Truth, either we are "His surrogates / Or betrayers." Some Muslims, Jews, and others might say essentially the same thing about their own religion. Influenced by the commonly shared Old Testament, the Western world, especially, has a penchant for this kind of approach to whatever the word "religion" means. Not a new idea, nothing tricky about it, just straight out in your face. I like that. Some Christians enjoy it as "scandalous." That's fine. That helps me know where I stand. And I respect Rifenburgh's conscience, conviction, and interpretation. I stand with his "Opposite Number in Samarkand," and I am proud of it. Rifenburg's subject is as fit for poetry as anything else, and I don't find it offensive, just out of touch with all of human history and religious experience, especially the last five-hundred years, and since the Enlightenment. Both religious and secular exclusivisms do that to people. They can keep people isolated from other equally valid traditions of the meaning and purpose of life, often not that different at the core from Christianity or an enlightened humanism, if one can be fair and open about it, make the brotherly effort to understand. Rifenburgh exhibits no such openness but continues along the line of what he had stated in the first poem, "Parmenides was right, / None of this exists!" Many Christian denominations have wisely moderated their thinking and teaching beyond caustic, dismissive either/or's.

Writing off the history and religious experience of much of the world is perhaps not an entirely efficacious approach for any human being, especially a poet, who must be open to all that is human, if he is truly to serve the Muses, the daughters of Zeus, the sacred servants of All. Had Rifenburgh read Robert Hayden's poetry years ago he would have found a much more open and universal perspective on life than he has spent his minor talent on. Toward universality, not exclusivism, is where the Divine Being, the Lord of history, has been guiding, and continues to guide, humankind. All peoples are able. In the light of the fullness of the literary tradition, which includes all nations and peoples, poets should encourage humanity to choose to travel together and be tolerant of their fellow human beings. We are all human, fallible, and not a one of us has ever had, or ever will have, the entire Truth, though it is human to think otherwise. At a time when it can seem some people in the United States and elsewhere are pushing toward Christian fascism or secular Utopia, it might help to step back from the brink and reflect on the healthy effect that pluralism and tolerance have had on civilization. People around our small planet need to value pluralism and universality more, not less.

Interview of the Author of *The Bower of Nil: A Narrative Poem*[4]
2002

Orrin Judd: Thank you for taking the time to answer a few questions. I enjoyed The Bower of Nil *and just wanted to ask about your writing and the ideas you express in this particular poem.*

On your website you say that: "After growing increasingly disaffected with academic literary culture, especially the Marxist antics of deconstruction and the alienated, poète maudit *mentality, [you] resigned from university teaching in 1996 and began a career in real estate, having now sold over eighteen million dollars worth of 'bourgeois property.'" That seems to resonate with the criticisms that Dana Gioia made in his essay "Can Poetry Matter?" in* The Atlantic Monthly.

Frederick Glaysher: Only coincidentally. Many writers articulated displeasure with academia and MFA poetry prior to Dana Gioia's article of 1991. Saul Bellow, Czeslaw Milosz, Joseph Epstein, Alvin Kernan, to mention only a few. Gioia's article struck me at the time as a fair statement but already old hat. Yet he shook the temple walls.

I found much of the ire he provoked quite amusing and confirming. I studied privately with Robert Hayden as early as 1979 partly because I was interested in his writing about American and Black history, subjects outside the self of postmodern obsession. I consciously chose at the time not to go the MFA route. The other day I looked at a copy of *Poets & Writers* and couldn't believe how many display ads were in it for MFA programs. In my essays, in little magazines as early as 1985, I was already struggling to chart a different course. Early on, Robert Frost had been a powerful influence on my approach

---

[4]*BrothersJudd*

to writing, an example of patient perseverance and independence. My master's thesis was on Edwin Arlington Robinson, another loner, of sorts.

I'd had a class in 1980, at the University of Michigan, in deconstruction, when it was just becoming the new and hot thing. I found it quite repulsive, Marxist, and decadent, from every perspective, intellectual, aesthetic, moral, whatever, and said so openly in class and in my papers, receiving a "C," the grade I'm the proudest of from my alma mater. My preface to *Into the Ruins* predates Gioia's manifesto.

Do you think your own poetry is different now that you're out of the academic hothouse and don't have to "publish or perish"?

My poetry was different while I was in it, which was part of the problem, so I don't see now what difference how I earn a livelihood should make. Gioia overemphasizes that, in my view. The problems of modernity and postmodernism are not merely related to how we earn our daily bread. And a mere return to meter and rhyme will in the end amount to nothing.

Do you feel like you can write things now that you couldn't have in that environment?

There really isn't much freedom of speech and conscience allowed in university departments. The phenomenon has been widely remarked upon and documented increasingly for over a decade by Alan Kors, David Horowitz, and others. It's been herd-think for a very long time, if not by its very structure and definition. My own experiences in a number of colleges and universities impressed that upon me in ways I needn't elaborate. Suffice it to say, I reached a point in my writing that I became convinced I could find more time and peace of mind outside the academic world than within it. That has very much proven to be the case, beyond anything I was able to imagine while teaching.

171

I long ago lost all respect for the campus and its tawdry radical politics, agendas. On all sides, we've fallen into faction, few willing to listen to and allow views other than their own, with often no real debate taking place.

Given that you're now pursuing a non-literary career too, how do you go about writing? Do you have an established schedule? or do you write only when inspired?

I've never been the kind of mill that gets up each morning and churns out another poem on schedule, though most of my writing has always been done in the mornings. I usually wake up about 5:30 am and write or read until about 11:00 or 12:00, seldom later. The rest of the day has always been when I tried to teach classes, take out the garbage, attend to all the mundane necessities of life. Real estate now provides me with a very flexible schedule. People seldom buy a house in the morning. Much preferable to grading piles of student papers, for not even nickels and dimes, I might add. As an independent entrepreneur, I have complete control over my time, working when I need to in order to support my family and my writing. The romantic, Bohemian idealization of the writer is quite flawed, though I've lived it too.

I'm basically a religious, moral soul. Writing crystallizes moments of consciousness, spiritual struggle for clarification, growth, and understanding, often, always really, won at only great cost and effort. My avowed goal has been to write relatively few poems but ones that I hope are worthy of the time of my fellow citizens. It seems to me many poets simply write too much and have nothing significant to say.

Where do you write and how do you write? Do you have a set room you use? Do you write longhand or type or use a PC?

I took up the computer early when it became widely available

172

in the late '80s. But my poems have always been written longhand, pencil or pen, with much revision before committing to type. I feel once I type up a poem it's more difficult to revise. Initially, on paper, I'm more free to sculpt and shape as need be. My prose, too, I usually write first on paper. It's important to me that the technology not break my train of thought once I get going, and computer bugs have a way of always intervening at the wrong moment. The real struggle and battles of writing are spiritual and intellectual. The current hardware is not important. Wherever I've lived, I've usually had a separate room or study to write in, though I've not always been able to afford the luxury, and at times had to work in a bedroom in order to keep writing.

In Bower of Nil, *Peter Marsh's wife has just been murdered and you recount a long night of philosophical and spiritual struggle that follows this tragedy. Without getting more personal than you might care to go, are you writing from some kind of personal experience of loss here? Or was it important to you for other reasons that Marsh have suffered this kind of loss? If not the loss itself, is the struggle he goes through something you've undergone?*

Yes, I'm writing from personal experiences of loss. There are literal and symbolic dimensions. For Peter Marsh, the gods send him the suffering he requires. I'd like to leave it at that.

Your bio notes that you've lived and taught in Japan, studied in China, with further formal study of India, lived on an Indian reservation, yet throughout the poem, and especially in the middle section, your source material is heavily Western and you've a pronounced Western viewpoint. Is the crisis that you speak of confined to the West? Or is the East not even caught up to the point where it can have undergone a decline yet?

I have a complicated history, I suppose, one that's difficult to compress into a dust jacket blurb, yet, I should acknowledge, is crucial to what I've written and why. I grew up in suburban Detroit, with some of my family living in the inner city. My genealogy is very much a part of my spiritual and literary consciousness, part of what compels me to confront and write about some of the things I do. My people come from England and Croatia, with deep roots in the Anglican and Catholic churches, with others from Germany, Ireland, and French Huguenots. Like many Americans, I lived and breathed social change and dislocation before I even began to develop intellectually, began to understand from what I was made. Much of my study and teaching has been, or was, of American and international literatures, non-Western. Their stories too are of social convulsion and change, spiritual upheaval, fragmentation. The modern human story.

Looking back, I was blessed to have had two experiences in high school, ages ago. One, I participated in a model United Nations day that set me on a path that continues to have resonance. Second, I had a class in world religions that opened up the range of transcendent experience and sent me off on many years of study down many paths. The interplay of the traditional and modern has always fascinated me. I've been drawn to or sought it out in all the great literatures and writers, East and West. Many take it for granted in Western literature, without realizing how central it is too, in, say, Asian literature and experience. I'd like to think Peter Marsh and David Emerson touch feelingly on these global matters of the human soul.

My essays, some still unpublished, though I hope forthcoming next year, discuss Asian literature much more in concrete detail.

I should say too that Rochester, the city I grew up in and returned to in 1994, is very important to my writing and consciousness. It's one of the few Detroit suburbs with a vital historic downtown, everyday representations of the past. It used

174

to be the country and thoroughly white, but has become one of the most "upscale" suburbs of Detroit, quite international and diverse. Rochester typifies for me all the changes and problems of postmodernity. I've lived and inhaled this atmosphere all my life. Late postmodern secular materialism, its rarefied air. I've seen a fair part of the world and country. Rochester's my hometown, my touchstone. I've never been a deracinated intellectual. My roots extend everywhere into Michigan and Rochester. I could tell you more about the history of our little town than you'd care to hear. And I can tell you where my family are buried. I regularly visit and tend their graves.

I've been surprised at times how the real estate business has served my literary interests, revealing the inner-most sanctum of people's lives, how they live, what they believe, incredibly different walks of life. It's all there in an instant for those who have eyes. The evanescent soul made manifest. Struggling under the confines of time. I feel it as a privilege, imposing a burden of respect, to have such access to the human heart of my fellow citizens. Unbeknownst, though it be. Largely a bedroom community for many international companies, the commissions in this city do a lot for a poet who wants to loaf and invite his soul. John Milton, it might be recalled, was taught by his father the family business of property management and the extending of loans, which enabled him to live on and increase his inheritance for most of his life, earning during one two-year period £300, a fortune for his day, until falling on hard times at the end. Anyway, I become perhaps too practical for some, violating sacred clichés of romanticism and university life.

In that middle portion, which I found the strongest part of the poem, you sound like a cultural conservative—is that a fair assessment?

Liberal and conservative tags and abstractions really have very little meaning to me. They are political and secular historical constructs that fail to represent my inmost being. So I always rankle at them both, loathe all party platforms. Politically, I've always been an independent. In every other sense as well. Group-thinking is very dangerous, whether academic, religious, literary, whatever. All organizations and religions tend to become oppressive to the individual human soul.

Those qualifications aside, I understand your point. I was baptized, raised, and confirmed a Catholic, and I genuinely respect the Church, the Pope, and the social and transcendent order and teachings of Christianity. Marx, and murderers like him, have never been my cup of tea. What Jonathan Swift called "prognosticators" have been the scourge of modern times. I believe many of our cultural problems are fundamentally spiritual and moral problems, heresy among academicians these days. On the other hand, Christians who regard the United Nations as the anti-Christ, and so forth, aren't my cup of tea either. Moderation in all things is the old saw we should all do more to reinvigorate.

Yet in the final section, when Peter Marsh begins to imagine how the pathologies of our age will be healed, you emphasize the advent of World Government and the value of the UN and internationalist institutions, so you sound like a Wilsonian liberal—is there such a dichotomy in your views?

Our time is one of politicization on all sides. We get it in the media, alas, the classroom, everywhere. *The Bower of Nil* is a poem, first and foremost. Poetry is mimesis. Poetry is a form of consciousness, of knowledge, a way of thinking, the reflection of consciousness, awareness, in words, language. Peter Marsh is a modern soul.

If the traditional West—the dissipation of which you lament—laid the groundwork for the kind of humane and democratic world governance you imagine will come, but most of the world has never undergone such Westernization, isn't this world government necessarily still a long way in our future?

When I was at the University of Michigan in the late '70s and early '80s, there was no curriculum that would allow me to study what I was drawn to. I had to patch together my own degree under the rubric of a Bachelor of General Studies—Biblical, Old Testament studies, Islamic, and world literature and history, with large swaths of Asian. Eventually, multi-culturalism and interdisciplinary studies caught up, in a sense, though much radicalized, in my view. It may be that the best answer to your question is to send those interested to my literary essay "The Victory of World Governance," available on my website, the culmination of my reading over 200 books on the League of Nations and the United Nations.

In the meantime, why is it appropriate for the democratic West to participate in institutions like the UN which include brutally repressive regimes like Syria, Burma, China, Cuba, etc.?

After my first book *Into the Ruins* was published in 1999, I gave over 230 radio interviews all over the country about my book and the United Nations. Many podunk stations in Idaho, North Dakota, elsewhere, as well as million-plus audiences in New York, Los Angeles, and so on. I learnt a great deal from the arduous experience. A few were recorded and are also on my website.

The poem includes a Baha'i prayer and you maintain a website (The Baha'i Faith & Religious Freedom of Conscience) about the Baha'i Faith, but the website [fglaysher.com/bahaicensorship] *refers to what seem to be bitter divisions within the faith. Do you consider yourself to be an adherent of the Baha'i faith? How did you become interested in the Baha'i faith? What beliefs does the faith entail? Is the poem informed by such faith? Or other religious faiths?*

I converted to the Baha'i Faith in 1976.[5] As with Christianity, human beings have various views on assorted controversial matters. The Baha'i Faith too has a complicated history, complicated all the more by its relative obscurity and the lack of reliable sources. I hope my Baha'i website remedies some deficiencies in that regard. The *via negativa* is an old Christian form, found, actually, in many religions.

During high school I became aware that something had happened to religion and belief in the modern world. My reading of the Bible and the scriptures of the great religions led me to recognize the transcendent had taken many forms in past human experience, expressed itself through many channels. I respect and affirm the oneness of that experience, the central Bahai teaching. I realize some dismiss the universality of transcendence as Gnosticism or whatever. At forty-eight, with more than half a lifetime of study and reflection, I know all the arguments and counter-arguments and wish not to fall into polemics or an apologia. I speak only for the integrity of my own conscience.

Are you working on a new project or projects? Can you tell us something about them?

---

[5]I consider myself a member of all religions, including the Reform Bahai Faith, an unorganized, universal interpretation of the Bahai writings and world religion, open to the truth of every spiritual and wisdom tradition. If that causes readers to think of a box, erase the box for an approximation, or read *Letters from the American Desert: Signposts of a Journey,* A Vision (2008).

Well (with a laugh), I worked for nearly twenty years on *Into the Ruins* and fifteen on *The Bower of Nil*, so I'm not the kind of poet who cranks out one book after another. I've always tended toward reading a hundred books to write a single line. However, I believe I'm almost done with a collection of essays, *The Grove of the Eumenides*, and hope to see it finally in print next year. I've begun writing too an epic poem, *The Parliament of Poets*. I've been thinking and making notes about it for over twenty years. If I'm able and allowed, it will probably take the rest of my life!

My Odyssey as an Epic Poet: Interview

Arthur McMaster: You published two books, within two years of each other, books that I find want to be read together. Your essays *The Myth of the Enlightenment* lays out the conditions for your fine epic poem *The Parliament of Poets*. Can you please tell us about how you came to take on such out-sized challenges?

Frederick Glaysher: Sure, I'd be happy to. Thank you, Arthur, for giving me the chance to speak with you and your readers, to put on record my odyssey as an epic poet.

Largely leaving aside my whole history of growing up an omnivorous reader, by the end of high school, I was already thinking of myself as a poet and regularly keeping a journal. I was especially already drawn to Robert Frost, including his prose, and other writers whose lives were marked by an independence of spirit, shall we say. When it came time to think about college, my intuition spoke emphatically that I had to take the road less traveled by or I'd end up like everybody else. It wasn't rational, rather deeply intuitive—a gut feeling that I couldn't fully articulate. But already I understood that the best writers were not made by universities. So while all my friends goose-stepped off to college, I chose to go off to an old farm in Oakland Township, Michigan, adjacent to where I grew up in Rochester. I spent a couple of years there reading and writing, trying to find my own voice. It was where I really read deeply into Walt Whitman and Emerson, and other poets that have remained essential to me throughout my life. Eventually, I felt I was ready to hold my own in a university, felt ready for it, needed it, and began my more conventional education, but I really became a poet on that farm.

Looking back now from over sixty years old, the writing of my epic poem finally behind me, I think another major threshold occurred in 1977 in a theater class that I took in Interpretative Reading. It was there I learned that the Greek rhapsodes would travel throughout Greece reciting Homer. I was thrilled by the idea, and it set me thinking. My experience in that class of performing a passage from William Wordsworth's "Michael" clinched it for me. Though overwhelmed and intimidated by the prospect, I began to consider writing an epic poem and then traveling around the world to recite it, reviving the ancient art of the Homer and rhapsodes. By 1982 I had written my first draft of a plot outline.

AM: And a fine major work it is, Frederick. I want to come back to the core idea, however, which challenges conventional thinking about man's "intellectual evolution," where spirituality is clearly a prime mover, but just now I would like to ask you to go back several years to your poetry influences. I know that you studied with Robert Hayden. What did his work mean to you, as a younger man?

FG: Without repeating too much what I say about Robert Hayden in the three essays that I have already written about him, in my books *The Grove of the Eumenides* and *The Myth of the Enlightenment*, I would say, yes, studying with Hayden was transformational, all the more for me since Hayden himself, when he was a young poet in the 1940s, had studied with W. H. Auden at the University of Michigan. I was very much taken then with T. S. Eliot and W. H. Auden, and that personal connection to the Tradition, if you will, has always meant a lot to me. Still does. On the other hand, I have found that people often want to read my biography too much in terms of Robert Hayden. I had been thinking of myself as a poet and studying and writing for at least eight years before I had ever met Hayden. So while I am the first one to say I owe him a lot, I don't owe him everything. In fact there were many things about my biography and intellectual interests that he never understood, couldn't understand, even wrongly advised me about, yet such things proved exactly what enabled me to write my epic poem.

Again, the strength of my independence and self-reliance saved me.

AM: Let's go to your more recent work, *The Myth of the Enlightenment*, and I love the implications from that title, what part of that research and writing are you most proud of?

FG: *The Myth of the Enlightenment* draws from a very long undercurrent of study in my first book of essays *The Grove of the Eumenides*. I'm really building on and extending from that first book of prose, bringing many themes to fruition. So, to my mind, *The Myth* represents my arduous struggle to bring into unity and coherence the diverse strands of my life-long intellectual and spiritual psychomachia, with East and West, represented, say, by Tolstoy, Milton, Tagore, and Saul Bellow, among others. Part of all that is the struggle of traditional conceptions of life and religion with modernity, ranging over the last five hundred years, and longer, with what Czeslaw Milosz insightfully called "the fad of nihilism," and Bellow scathingly referred to as "knee-jerk nihilism," my opponent throughout all my books. In *The Parliament of Poets* and *The Myth of the Enlightenment*, I believe I have slain that Beast, and hope, in time, word will spread, and my books will find readers who can recognize and understand the importance of that victory. The historical record demonstrates that all recorded civilizations have been capable of major transformation in the past when essential to save themselves. Those that were incapable of such epochal shifts destroyed themselves and passed into oblivion. World civilization now stands in the balance.

AM: And now for the *piece de resistance*. Your epic poem *The Parliament of Poets* runs to some 290 pages—one poem. Epic indeed. And it is a striking volume. I would like to see more of this kind of serious work. We find mythology and folklore, such as Merlin, worked with so cleverly, but also biblical antecedents and other, related, creation myths—I mention Baal—moving elegantly to such literary figures as Chaucer and Tolstoy. Throughout we find, pardon the cliché, man's inhumanity to man—the Russian Gulag... Help our PQ readers understand how you put it all together. The planning for this must have been daunting.

FG: Yes, it was daunting. Right from the beginning. In all honesty I was overwhelmed by the notion, taking on such a challenge, but, unbidden, the shaman call kept coming, the undeniable demand, that I, as Emerson wrote, which I once quoted to Robert Hayden, visibly shocking him, "Say, 'it is in me, and shall out.'" Looking back, I believe it was the independence of those years of solitary study that helped give me the necessary tenacity of spirit, as well as the intuitive sense to recognize that there was no other literary form in which I could fully express what I felt about life. Early on I realized that I had to go directly to the great epics and poets to learn how to write it. Although I had read by the mid Eighties several academic books on epic poetry, for the most part, they weren't helpful. I left them dissatisfied, except for E. M. W. Tillyard's book on epic poetry and one of his articles. That period of study culminated in my long essay "Epopee" in *The Grove of the Eumenides*, the last one in the book, looking to the future. I talk more about Tillyard in an Epic Poetry Workshop I gave at the Austin International Poetry Festival, in 2012, in a YouTube video.

AM: I suspect that few of our readers will recognize the name Tillyard. Can you help? Please go on.

FG: Unlike the New Criticism and other fads in criticism since, Tillyard was a real scholar worthy of the name, not a theorist or sophist, still largely in the old historical, humanistic, practical, useful mode of criticism. His scholarship was of crucial importance to me, for it helped me understand, at a fairly young age, what I was up against and how to proceed, go about actually studying for and writing an epic poem. I consider Tillyard an example of the role scholars have in building civilization, not tearing it down. There was no comparable help I ever found elsewhere. I was largely on my own and had to figure out almost everything for myself. In fact, I soon realized almost all of the prevailing scholarship and fads in culture and poetry would lead me astray from my chosen task, if I allowed it. By the early to mid Eighties I became aware that I was training my mind to the task of writing an epic poem. As Virgil had written three books, I paced myself from there on, deciding I would follow his example, writing a book of lyric poems and dramatic monologues, then a book-length narrative poem telling a longer story, working up to and leading to my ability to write an epic poem, with many personae. Similarly thinking of developing my narrative ability, I wrote my master's thesis on the narrative poems of Edwin Arlington Robinson.

AM: Can you tell us more about other influences?

FG: All of this, of course, was aside from the necessity of finding and achieving a Vision of our historical, global moment. Some of the great historians and scholars of religion and myth proved to be the most helpful, such as Arnold Toynbee's many works, most of which I've read, especially *Mankind and Mother Earth* and his Gifford Lecture on religion. Most of the books by Huston Smith, too, beginning even in the early Seventies, were very important, as was Joseph Campbell and Carl Jung. Instead of the linear approach of Virgil and Milton in the *in medias res*, I felt my recognition of Jung's formidable understanding of dreams and modern psychology required a more dream-like phantasmagoria, slightly "smudging" it, like a painter, with his thumb, toward the logic of dreams. And I, of course, read all the great epic poems, East and West, revising my notes and plot outline, again and again, over decades of study and reflection.

184

For many years I couldn't figure out how to start writing, wasn't ready. So I just kept reading and studying, following and trusting my desultory intuition to take me where needed, making notes, jotting down details and choice tidbits. Into my fifties, during the winter preceding my actually beginning to write in the early spring of 2008, I had a few key realizations that began to open the doors for me. I read somewhere that Virgil had first written out the Aeneid in prose and then polished it into verse. However apocryphal that may be, it made me realize I could do the same, coupled with the rhetorical strategy of outlining an essay or piece of oratory, epic plot in this case.

Instead of being shot out of a cannon or ascending to the moon tied to vials of hot air, as in Cyrano de Bergerac, and so forth, my life-long fascination with fairy tales, Mother Goose, and children's literature came to mind, along with Robert Hayden, solving the major problem that I struggled with for decades of how the Persona would get to the moon.

Another major insight came about when I read of a 19th Century American writer who wrote his best book when he made his own personal struggle to write it part of the story itself. I have always considered myself a fairly private person, solitary and loath to share much of my most personal life with strangers, so it was not easy to confront the possibility of sharing my inner-most self with the reader. I can't emphasize this enough. Though very painful for me, I think allowing the reader into my inner struggle to create an epic poem deepened it on many levels of meaning and nuance, and makes it hopefully much more engaging for the reader, for the Persona becomes archetypal, beyond my small self. I had to grow within to do that and my characters too had to grow, even, I'd like to think, in the vignettes, into the deepest psychic levels where I am truly trying to resolve the conundrums that I have brooded on all my life. I think and hope readers can feel that, for they also have that sacred place of consciousness.

185

Analogous to the importance of Virgil to me, Dante not only led to my realizing that I could meld his canto within the twelve-book form of Virgil and Milton, but also that his "deep structure," as I think of it, given near the end of Canto XVII of the *Paradiso*, "if it all be penned," would dovetail almost perfectly with my own more universal spiritual experience and outlook and struggle to affirm the universal, transcendent sovereignty of God, which came together with the Rose Image of Mother Earth. I watched Joseph Campbell's conversations with Bill Moyers when they were first broadcast, and many times thereafter, helping me to understand the Image of Earthrise, and read his articles on it.

As a global tale, I am speaking to the entire planet, not merely the Western world. While the whole is always more than the sum of its parts, I gratefully acknowledge my indebtedness to such writers and thinkers as Joseph Campbell, the historian Arnold Toynbee, Huston Smith, Aldous Huxley, Carl Jung, and many others of open and universal sensibility. Campbell, especially, wrote on shamanism and myth and their power to heal the tribe through a visionary experience and tale. Campbell also wrote repeatedly about the Earth rising above the horizon of the moon, as the great new mythic Symbol for our time. I hope that my epic tale might be judged worthy of the best in their thinking and work, and rise to the theme in my own way as a poet.

AM: Jung is so often at play in these highly intellectual inquiries. Can you speak to your sense of the spiritual?

FG: I first read Carl Jung in the early 1970s, *Man and His Symbols*, where many people start with Jung. His book *Answer to Job* and the essay "Psychology and Literature" also became very important to me. I repeatedly found myself going back to him, throughout my life. Writing my epic poem, there were times when I truly felt I was in something like a trance. The

Muse said "go in that direction," despite my rational plans, and I knew I could but obey, all the better for the poem. I think Jung is right, by implication, that the artist must surrender to that. Often I would read and study something for months and years, and then, inexplicably, cooking on the back burner, so to speak, something would come together, and there it was, just pouring out in a passage, a poem, a chunk of essay or whatever. I don't believe the rationalistic conceptions of the mind and soul do justice to what's involved.

All sanctimony aside, with all humility, as the descendant of Christians from several of the 60,000-plus denominations, from my first reading it in high school, I have always been moved by and savored the counsel of Christ to "pray to your Father" (Matt 6.6), and by, in the various great religions, similar guidance to pray and meditate, as in Rumi, Kabir, St. John of the Cross, Meister Eckhart, *The Cloud of Unknowing*, Thomas Merton, Buddhism, and so on. Not long after high school, I found myself drawn to prayer and meditation, usually morning and evening, already when I was in my early twenties, often back then for an hour or two a day, though the more sober "householder" stage of life necessarily shortened that. As usual, I prayed daily throughout the years of writing my epic, often turning to God, asking for help and guidance, meditating on how to proceed, resolving many literary problems through prayer. Prayer and meditation have been and are still important parts of my life as a man and a poet. There is a Mystery in consciousness, and in prayer we can experience it. I believe prayer is essential to develop the deepest levels in ourselves of what it means to be a human being, our deepest levels of consciousness. Naturally, all this is reflected in my epic poem. I hope this conveys somewhat how I grappled with actually writing my epic.

AM: Thank you. I want to take you to a question that should let you vent a bit about American poetry today and your observations on current themes in that poetry. You sir are not a conventional poet. I know that you have taught poetry, but I sense that you see yourself as somewhat of an outrider. Is that fair? Will you comment?

FG: Yes, from my earliest years, I've always thought of myself in opposition to much of what has become the prevailing, conventional modes of literary and cultural thinking and writing, academic and otherwise, without even trying, to my mind, and very much beyond postmodernism and all its clichés and assumptions. Part of it stems from my early interest in world religions and in the United Nations, my life-long study of history, East and West, all of which began in high school. I've gone deeper and deeper into both ever since, in terms of literature, history, spiritual outlook, evermore what I think of as universality, while I fear much of the culture, around the world, has become more insular, parochial, closed off, superficial, and self-obsessed with backward, retrograde flights into imaginary pasts, which plague us, or has sunk into nihilistic and secular modes of thinking and utopias. Nihilism is an extremely dangerous, dehumanizing reduction of the fullness of life, of the 200,000 years of *Homo sapiens* on this planet. I consider it more of a threat than even fanatical Islam. We must not fail to understand and remember that dis-eased, nihilistic rationalism, along with its companion materialism, has produced the most oppressive, bloodiest episodes of the last hundred years.

AM: Good point. How has the work been received?

FG: I'm grateful that a fair number of people have read and reviewed my epic around the world and have responded very favorably. I have at times been surprised to find that some readers respond only to one chapter or another of my epic and its respective worldview, respond only to the exclusivism which they already hold or value, while not perhaps hearing the full symphony, what I'd like to think is a song of the fullness of human existence itself. I suppose that stands to reason, so to speak, and indicates somewhat where and how we human beings still need to grow and evolve, are evolving. In our age of extreme, even ridiculous specialization, many know little outside their box, cutting them off from the plenitude and complexity of life, substituting narrow, dehumanizing ideologies. In this way nihilism has us in a stranglehold.

So, in an age of Balkanization and fragmentation, I have always sought unity, what might bring the disparate parts together, harmonize what divides and threatens humanity, through the Supreme Power of the Imagination, our most distinctively human capacity. I still cling to my life-long hope that a global, universal epic tale might help heal the wounds of modernity sufficiently to make the difference, before it is too late. In our corrosively cynical, fragmented state, it can seem most fail to have the imagination to appreciate the possibility. I continue to hope that a point will be reached at which that will begin to change. The Power of Art to reach and touch the souls of humankind must not be neglected and dismissed. Art is the language of the gods.

As to my experience with Academia, I've repeatedly left the university, found it unconducive to my intellectual and spiritual development and growth, which has always been very painstakingly slow and hard won. Because I understood early on that the university doesn't own or represent the Tradition, I've always been able to walk away from it when necessary, what I consider five times, last in 1996. I've always felt that much of the university has lost and betrayed the Tradition.

AM: I cannot let you go without asking this next one, in my assumption that you are a deeply contemplative poet: what are you working on now?

FG: For a long time, and especially the last two or three months, I've been thinking again about writing an essay tentatively titled

"Quantum Physics and Poetry." I feel there's a need perhaps to spell out in prose some of what I'm writing about in my epic poem, to help the reader, as Whitman said. I first read about Quantum Physics in about 1973 in a book by George Leonard, called *The Transformation*, and then went on to Thomas Kuhn's *The Structure of Scientific Revolutions*, reading many other works through the years. In my epic, of course, I wasn't writing a science textbook, but, I'd like to think, absorbed and synthesized some of the implications of Quantum Physics, at very deep metaphorical and metaphysical levels, to reach into the human psyche.

I believe Quantum Physics changes the nature and meaning of all of the traditional religious and spiritual terms, which is very difficult to convey to people. I fear it may take another five hundred years and sheer hell for humanity fully to understand. Modernity has left people often exceedingly distraught over religion when such need not be the case. Minds on all sides tend to be indoctrinated and snap shut before understanding can even begin to take place, as Allan Bloom understood. I do address Quantum Physics in my epic, in what I think is the best way, in the language and epistemology of poetry, though also in *The Myth of the Enlightenment*. I've been thinking, too, for quite a while now of writing an essay on Dante and Cervantes, in terms of their own engagement with Islam.

To my surprise in late 2013, I had the startling thought of writing another epic poem, which had never occurred to me before, so intent was I on *The Parliament*, though more of a dramatic narrative, perhaps somewhat like John Milton's *Samson Agonistes*. Having spent over thirty years on *The Parliament of Poets*, I doubt I have enough time left for another full-scale epic (laughing).

And then on a shorter time-scale, I still hope to live out that rhapsode dream, at least a little, maybe for a few years, if I'm lucky, somehow, though in this world, at my age, I know many dreams never come true, but serve to inspire us toward our better angels. No matter what happens, I'm grateful that I have been allowed to finish my epic. I feel fulfilled as a man that that dream has come true.

III   Race in America

Robert Hayden's Angle of Ascent[6]

Emphasizing the continuing influence of Robert Hayden, Phillip M. Richards of Colgate University, educated at Yale University and the University of Chicago, writes, in his 2006 book, *Black Heart: The Moral Life of Recent African American Letters*, "In the long view of African-American poetry, Hayden's symbolist poetry has proved more influential than the Black Arts movement.... Hayden, years after his death, remains our most influential black poet, and his followers the most productive and distinguished school of artist intellectuals" (178). Similarly, Charles Henry Rowell, editor of the journal *Callaloo*, in his book published last year, *Angles of Ascent: A Norton Anthology of Contemporary African American Poetry*, writes, "The title of this anthology . . . pays tribute to Hayden, a master artist who left behind an extraordinary gift in the pantheon of North American poetry."

I want to emphasize what Charles Henry Rowell is implying by his carefully choosing the words "North American Poetry." Rowell understands the literary, social, and aesthetic values that Hayden stood for and realized he couldn't narrow them down. I myself read Robert Hayden's poetry for years before I became one of Hayden's students in 1979. While fully recognizing and relishing Hayden's poetry, then and now, as I believe the foremost engagement with African-American experience in poetry, I've always had the sense, too, which Rowell suggests, that Hayden's poetry speaks to the human experience of all North Americans, with the universal aspirations of the greatest poets, such as a Whitman. As the author of an epic poem in which Robert Hayden is a character, that has been reviewed in

---

[6]Presented at the Robert Hayden/ Dudley Randall Centennial Symposium, Wayne State University, April 2, 2014. On April 3, I read the canto "The Flight to the Moon."

Poetry Cornwall in England as "a masterpiece that will stand the test of time," and reviewed by Dr. Hans-George Ruprecht of Carleton University in Ottawa as "a great epic poem of startling originality and universal significance," I gratefully acknowledge that I could never have written my epic poem, *The Parliament of Poets*, without the example of the art and tutelage of Robert Hayden. Today, we honor Robert Hayden's striving for the universal, his ability to help us see and understand that about ourselves and our nation, our national experience, one of the perennial goals of great art. At a time when the goals and scope of the literary art were becoming smaller and smaller, turning inward on the small experience of the confessional postmodern self, all the clichés of the personal, the deriding of so-called meta-narratives, Robert Hayden unabashedly saw the personal against the backdrop of a wider social canvas, ever increasingly global in his reach, leading to his poem "[American Journal]," the cosmic vision of his persona from an alien civilization, more human than we are, pondering the nature of life in the United States, broadening out to the entire planet.

By Hayden's own self-assessment, the arc or trajectory of his life was painstakingly slow, and would include among its highlights, as a brief sketch, his birth in 1913 and growing up in Detroit's Paradise Valley, his years at Detroit City College, now this institution, Wayne State University, writing theatre reviews for the Michigan Chronicle and radio plays in Windsor, for the WPA "A History of the Negro in Michigan," eventually studying at the University of Michigan, first as a part-time student and then full-time, earning a master's degree in English, and staying on for a few years as a teaching assistant. His taking W. H. Auden's class, The Analysis of Poetry, was a crucial experience for him and helped further open up for Hayden a wider understanding of the art of poetry and the role of the poet that he sought to serve the rest of his life, no matter how fierce the chorus became for him to return to his earlier, less intellectually sophisticated folk style of the 1930s. At Fisk University for decades, overburdened with teaching as many as five courses a semester, Hayden somehow still continued slowly to write remarkable poetry that accumulated into his early books, poetry of striking moral, spiritual, and aesthetic vision. Although there were many encouraging signs for Hayden throughout his life, he often felt he was, with some justification, as he was once called, "the best unknown poet in America." No account of his life can leave out the irony that in the same year, 1966, he received the Grand Prize for Poetry at the First World Festival of Negro Arts in Senegal, Africa (reportedly attended by ten-thousand people, a Who's Who of African and African-American literature), personally presented to Hayden in New York by President and poet Léopold Sédar Senghor, and was attacked at the Black Writers Conference at Fisk University, antinomies enough to shake up and test the soul of any poet, causing Hayden to weigh ever more carefully what he really believed. The complexity around race for Robert Hayden goes right to the heart of the matter, of what does it mean to be human and an American, recalling the reflections of the early American French farmer Crèvecœur, the perennial struggle of "life upon these shores." The son of a father of African origin and a mother of Irish, Hayden found himself torn between his natural love for his parents and a society that often failed to affirm who he was in terms of his full humanity. On more than one occasion, Hayden made clear to me that he had experienced racist attitudes from both blacks and whites. Thirty-four years after his death, we Americans still have much to learn from Robert Hayden, though, arguably, we've made significant progress on race, not to be lost sight of.

In an interview with Alvin Aubert, Jr., in 1975, Hayden responds to many of the issues involved with race for him by saying, in perhaps his clearest statement of what he believed, "to advocate or to support separatism in any form is to give aid and comfort to the bigots." Hayden goes on to criticize the tendency to pull away or back, self-segregate. Phillip Richards, in his courageous and important book *Black Heart*, insightfully discusses in extensive detail the dynamics involved. Richards' chapter on Hayden is one of the most insightful essays I've ever read about him, emphasizing Hayden was more universal than Baha'i. Hayden once told me that as a graduate student at the University of Michigan he had had to live a significant distance away from campus, out in the area of Ann Arbor where most blacks of the time were forced to live. He said he hated it and wanted to live in the dormitories with other students but couldn't. Such experiences are behind his saying to Aubert, "I think the 'Toms' are the ones who are running around being separate, running around college campuses wanting their own dormitories and their own cafeterias and so on." Notice, there's nothing there about the Baha'i Faith. It's all right out of lived experience, and lays out his thinking in clear and stark opposition to the louder voices of the Black Arts Movement, supposedly avant garde. Closing the topic with Aubert, Hayden stated, "If we're in separate dormitories and classrooms, then we don't have to be dealt with. So that's my answer to that." To look at all of it in another way, Hayden understood both that the Black Arts Movement was a coterie, which by literary definition always involves some form of the narrowing of vision, separatism from the fullness of life, and a form of romanticism, as Richards' book discusses. To Hayden, this coterie emphatically had potentially devastating social and cultural consequences. His wisdom in this regard has been proven by time.

In 1975, Hayden had already been back in Ann Arbor for five years, even a little longer as a visiting professor, and was about to become the first poet of black heritage to be the Consultant in Poetry at The Library of Congress, to which he was reappointed for a second term, an honor in itself which doesn't always happen. Looking back at Hayden's development as a poet from our vantage point, his career can look more like that of a poet who made slow but steady progress, hard won every inch of the way, or one should say, earned by the struggle and sweat of his own brow. Another way of phrasing it, is that Hayden had to struggle to find readers who could understand him, a struggle that in some ways continues, as it does for every great poet, as layer upon layer unfolds over time. All of which brings to mind the poet Samuel Johnson's observation on Shakespeare about how he had managed to write so many plays, in a word, Johnson wrote, "perseverance."

I need to touch briefly on some of my own personal biography in order to comment further on Hayden. I was born in 1954 at the old Evangelical Deaconess Hospital on East Jefferson Avenue, my family living at the time in the vicinity of Jefferson Chalmers, where some had for generations. Growing up I had many experiences of downtown Detroit, shopping at the old Hudsons, Cadillac Square, and so on. Although my parents moved to the suburbs, we always regularly visited relatives in Jefferson Chalmers, who owned the Essex Bakery, on Essex Street. All that and more was always in my own consciousness of who I was as someone growing up in the Detroit area. As a young person in late high school, I was a counselor at Camp Ozanam, run by the Society of St. Vincent de Paul, largely to give inner city kids a chance to get out in the country during the summer, and later I was a Childcare Worker for a year at the Detroit Baptist Children's Home for emotionally impaired children on 13 Mile and Evergreen, while living in Detroit near Seven Mile and John R, frequently using the Detroit Public Library, where I first read a poster about the poet Robert Hayden. Through all that, I was always involved, as many, if not most, Detroiters are, with people from all backgrounds. I learned from life experience the truth that Dudley Randall once recalled in an interview that he had been taught by his own parents, that there are good and bad people from both races. I cared for and about the young boys in my charge from the inner city just as much as from anywhere else, just as much as the emotionally impaired children, black and white, from families that had often failed them. As a student at Oakland Community College, before transferring to Eastern Michigan University, and then the University of Michigan, I had classes with people of all backgrounds and walks of life who studied, sacrificed, and worked hard to change the course of their own lives. I've often recalled Hayden saying to me once, criticizing what seemed to him to be the changing moral landscape, that when he was growing up, "There was no shame in being poor but respectable," a truth perhaps our time has too often forgotten. All this and more was part of why Hayden and I clicked. I think now he understood more than I did, as a young poet intent on his own obsessions, how our paths were merging.

Often in history, cities, East and West even, have marked major turns in direction, or encouraged them, through the dedication of new civic symbols and statues, helping people to have a visible sign of change, renewal, the direction in which to go or strive. About a year ago, walking out the back entrance of the Detroit Public Library, the thought occurred to me that the large island of the circle drive, having nothing but grass on it, facing Wayne State University, would be a most suitable place for a bronze statue of Robert Hayden, a visible sign of the values of knowledge and learning that he represented and had lived his life for, the young poet who studied at both the public library and now adjacent university as it has expanded. Recall that it was at the Detroit Public Library that a librarian in the 1930s would set aside books of poetry for him knowing his interest in the art. Facing the campus of Wayne State University, it would honor and highlight the importance of both institutions as well as the example of a man and poet who was the offspring of both. I gladly share what for me has become a persistent idea with anyone willing to consider making it a reality. If there's any poet from Detroit and Michigan worthy of the honor, it's Robert Hayden. The arc of Robert Hayden's ascent is still rising.

In the poem "For a Young Artist," Hayden turns biography into myth, one might say as every great poet does. Inspired by a short story by Gabriel Garcia Marquez, Hayden transforms the plot into the arduous ascent of the artist, through trial and tribulation, misunderstanding, if not antagonism, to the realization of his deepest aspirations and visions, an almost Jungian myth of the process of individuation. (ending with a reading of the poem)

> Sprawled in the pigsty,
>> snouts nudging snuffling him—
> a naked old man
>> with bloodstained wings...

A Courageous Man and a Brilliant Book
2000

In *Creating Equal*, Ward Connerly returns the *human* dimension to the realities of race in America. Where so often what the poet Robert Hayden called "race rhetoric" substitutes for thought and dialogue, Connerly confronts long-held affirmative action doctrine with compelling insight into the pervasive devastation race preferences have actually had for all people. His emphasis on the necessity of basic human virtue and morality stands as both an indictment of us all and a call to struggle together toward a new vision of what it means to be an American.

At last someone other than a radical black or white "civil rights professional" has found a way to speak to these issues and reach all Americans—not merely the campus crowd.

Connerly rightly deserves to be more widely known not merely as an opponent of race preferences but rather as a matchless defender of free speech and conscience, a cause for which he has also suffered dearly at one university after another throughout our country.

Whatever shape our future will take regarding race, Ward Connerly's personal and public odyssey will be part of the answer, as it is a clear sign for renewed hope that reason and sanity may yet prevail.

Enough: The Phony Leaders, Dead-End Movements, and Culture of Failure that are Undermining Black America—and What We Can Do About It
2006

The major shortcoming of Juan Williams book is that he doesn't go far enough. But more of that later. It should first be said that he goes very far indeed, saying much that has needed to be said for years, if not decades. No mean achievement. The subtitle itself sets out much of the structure of the book. Williams' discussion is built around Bill Cosby's speech in 2004 on the fiftieth anniversary of the Supreme Court's decision in Brown v. Board of Education, as well as Cosby's numerous other talks throughout the country since then, including Detroit.

Williams laments the lack of any real leaders in the black community in the tradition of Frederick Douglass, Booker T. Washington, W. E. B. Dubois, and Martin Luther King, Jr., all of whom, in Williams' view, shared a commitment to black self-reliance and self-determination:

> In its place is a tired rant by civil rights leaders about the power of white people—what white people have done wrong, what white people didn't do, and what white people should do. This rant puts black people in the role of hapless victims waiting for only one thing—white guilt to bail them out (32).

He lambasts both Jesse Jackson and Al Sharpton as never having really accomplished much, in a way similar to John McWhorter's scathing reference to "black theatrics." Returning often to Bill Cosby's speeches, concurring with Cosby, Williams states, "At some point, people have to take a personal accounting, turn away from any self-defeating behavior, and be sure they are doing everything in their power to put their families and their communities in a position to prosper and advance" (43). Jackson and Sharpton have "slowed the emergence of any new model of national black political leadership" (47). Juan Williams never suggests that Bill Cosby is in a sense the model—Cosby himself has repeatedly stated he's an entertainer, not a leader, but merely someone sick and tired of it all and speaking out to wake people up to how bad things really are. Williams' book goes a long way towards helping people do just that by facing the unpleasant facts.

Some of those facts include the diversion of attention and resources from the truly pressing needs of the black community to a futile fight for reparations for slavery. The chapter title says it all: "The Reparations Mirage."

In a chapter on education, Juan Williams frames his discussion with Cosby's provocative challenge, "What the hell good is Brown v. Board of Education if nobody wants it?" The dismal statistic of a 50 percent black drop out rate from high school, the best students pilloried as "acting white," behavior way out of control, and so on, all adds up to deep and endemic crisis for young black people and the community. Cosby, Williams, and others are to be applauded for caring enough about the students themselves that they have publicly confronted and discussed what the issues really are, unlike those who, as Cosby cuts to the quick, are worried "they would lose their gig." Indeed, there are black leaders and school officials who deserve to, and should, lose their "gig," for the sake of the children and the future good of the black community.

On the national level in regard to black crime, Juan Williams similarly asserts there has been a failure of leadership:

> Never a word was spoken about the need for black Americans to take up their own war on drugs and on crime as a matter of personal responsibility.... All the silence could not blind anyone to the neon lights flashing sad facts

about the severity of black crime. By 2004 federal data showed that black Americans—13 percent of the population— accounted for 37 percent of the violent crimes, 54 percent of arrests for robbery, and 51 percent of murders. Most of the victims of these violent criminals were their fellow black people. This legitimate fear of violent crime by black people spread into every corner of the nation (116).

To these sad facts, Cosby and Williams rightly emphasize the utter crisis that confronts black America, all of America, and the need to wake up, take personal responsibility, and begin at the most basic level of society, with rebuilding the black family and community, citing the past in about 1950 when 78% of black children were raised in two-parent homes, compared to today with approximately only 34%. Williams also repeatedly emphasizes Cosby's other major points, education and hard work, giving many inspiring examples.

Part of that rebuilding involves confronting the glorification of violence and sex in hip-hop and rap music and videos. Increasingly widely criticized, and justly, by many people, black and otherwise, for the misogyny and demeaning portrayals and exploitation of women, Williams discusses a number of disturbing and shocking incidents and rappers, highlighting that again black leaders, by failing to speak out and condemn "the corruption of rap for all these years" has "resulted in real damage to the most vulnerable of black America—poor children, boys and girls, often from broken homes" (133).

Throughout his book, Juan Williams demonstrates a firm command of the history of black people in America, the heroic struggle for freedom and dignity. Bringing it alive for black people today, he shows how black history is indeed relevant to the current problems of phony leadership and community crisis. He seems to be saying the resources are there in the past and in the people; we need to do a better job of drawing on the best and striving to live up to it; we need leaders who can set the right standards, point us in the right direction, and demand we struggle for the mountain top.

I would argue the psychological chains binding the wrists of the black community must be cut, if any true progress is to be made. After all, the Michigan Civil Rights Initiative (MCRI), up for a vote in the very same year Williams publishes his book, will almost certainly pass and quite probably help further lead to a nationwide end of racial preference. Williams ignores the entire issue. It seems to me that Ward Connerly, Shelby Steele, Thomas Sowell, and others are more perceptive in this regard, kicking the destructive, misbegotten crutch away. But for anyone interested in an insightful survey and analysis of the issues that will remain and must be confronted on November 8th, Juan Williams' *Enough* may be one of the best places to begin.

White Guilt: How Blacks and Whites Together Destroyed the Promise of the Civil Rights Era
2006

The 2006 approval by voters of the Michigan Civil Rights Initiative merely marks another step along the path of a much deeper cultural shift on the part of blacks and whites. The old formulas have not worked, are not working, and definitely never will work. In his book *White Guilt*, Shelby Steele tells us why, explains the sorry spectacle of over forty years of misguided government intervention in the lives of black people and the social devastation and erosion that "redemptive liberals," white and black, have wreaked upon a people, undermining their earlier comparable independence and social cohesion.

Shelby Steele clearly states the real problem of the black community is one of underdevelopment. Poor leadership has failed for decades to teach that "black Americans are capable of being fully responsible for their own advancement" (60). Elsewhere, in his Bradley Lecture, Steele remarks, "Our great mistake was to begin to rely on white guilt instead of ourselves." After the achievements of the 1960s civil rights leaders, who wanted individual rights, the new generation of black militants resorted to anger, pressure, and intimidation to stigmatize white society into a debilitating sense of guilt for the wrongs of slavery and Jim Crow in order to win concessions of monetary and social compensation. It worked. Both sides got what they wanted. A paltry coin. Release from stigma. But the Faustian bargain was at the expense, for many, of further self-development and self-reliance in the black community, leading to a worsening of the social problems that all peoples are prone to when they begin to blame others for their problems. Breaking out of this pernicious system is the challenge before us all.

Nowhere has the mutually destructive relationship been more blatant than in the policies of affirmative action:

> Preferential affirmative action, the classic 'results'-oriented racial reform, tells minorities quite explicitly that they will not have to compete on the same standards as whites precisely so they can be included in American institutions without in fact achieving the same level of excellence as whites. The true concern of 'results' reform is the moral authority of the institution. Minority development is sacrificed to the magnanimity of the institution (61).

As with the University of Michigan, so with all American institutions desperately seeking to distance and disassociate themselves from the racist white supremacy of the past. Steele's critique of such practices is utterly scathing, peeling back layer upon layer of corruption, duplicity, deceit, all carried out at the expense of young people, black, white, Asian, and so on. The institution is more interested in social engineering and proving to the world that it is not implicated in racism. Sacrificial lambs on all sides.

In his dissent to the decision of the other Supreme Court members in Grutter versus Bollinger, Justice Clarence Thomas quotes a passage from the abolitionist Frederick Douglass:

> What I ask for the negro is not benevolence, not pity, not sympathy, but simply justice. The American people have always been anxious to know what they shall do with us.... I have had but one answer from the beginning. Do nothing with us! Your doing with us has already played the mischief with us. Do nothing with us! ...And if the negro cannot stand on his own legs, let him fall also. All I ask is, give him a chance to stand on his own legs! Let him alone!

… [Y]our interference is doing him positive injury ("What the Black Man Wants," 1865).

Steele writes that the dissent of Justice Thomas, like that of Frederick Douglass, is a "fiery and indignant demand that blacks be seen and understood first of all as human beings" (144). Paternalism, by whatever American institution, the Supreme Court or the University of Michigan, constitutes a flagrant and intolerable injustice that sends waves of disruption down through the decades and generations, overwhelming and disrupting the development and dignity of a people, all people.

Shelby Steele's great book helps us to understand what has happened to us all and sets a new course away from the interfering good intentions that have led to extremely bad results. It is difficult to take the advice of Frederick Douglass. To do nothing. To trust in the innate capacities of human beings. To look to the individual to work out the meaning of his or her own destiny. To resist making ourselves feel good at the demeaning expense of others. Somehow we must learn a deeper meaning of justice, struggle together towards a deeper measure of understanding and life together as people, citizens, Americans, human beings. The wisdom of people like Shelby Steele and Justice Clarence Thomas will help us get there, tap into the deepest springs of human motivation and achievement.

Given Dr. Steele's experience teaching in university English departments, I found his critique of race and gender studies in literature and education particularly striking and perceptive of the sophistries involved, having myself met on many occasions his reform-minded academic "Betty," an educator full of misguided good intentions.

Shelby Steele's *White Guilt* is a book of such penetrating insight into the dynamics of black and white misfortune and lost opportunity that no person remotely interested in the racial issues of our time should fail to read it.

I should mention that *White Guilt* was part of the reading I did before my participation on a panel discussion about the Michigan Civil Rights Initiative (MCRI) at Wayne State University Law School, October 26, 2006, an account of which is in the book *Ending Racial Preferences: The Michigan Story*, 2008, by Carol M. Allen.[7] I highly recommend it for a comprehensive treatment of the issues involved.

---

[7]Lexington Books. Unindexed pages, 127-128, 130, 151-152.

Reawakening the Dream
2000

This morning, sometime around three or four AM, I woke up thinking about Shelby Steele's *A Dream Deferred: The Second Betrayal of Black Freedom in America*. I read it a number of months ago and have been wanting to write a brief note about it. There are so few intelligent, reasonable, sane voices speaking about racial matters in America I feel it as a duty to try to acknowledge those who are so scorned by the forces of both white and black extremist liberalism. The thought that impelled me out of bed was that I owe it to my memory of the best friend I've ever had in my life, who happened to be black, long deceased and sorely missed. So I struggle for words, knowing I will never meet that high mark. Others may criticize Mr. Steele for emphasizing this and underplaying that, but I want to praise his thoughtful probing of the dynamics of affirmative action and how it assuages white guilt while keeping some black people from developing their highest potential. As a former college English instructor, I occasionally had minority students who were accustomed to being handed A's and were shocked to receive C's. Repeated experience convinced me that affirmative action was part of the problem. They lacked the self-discipline and responsibility that Steele extolls: "Very often those who educate poor blacks feel excused from the responsibilities of high expectations and academic rigor by the very conditions that make such expectations mandatory."

My students had had years of misguided low expectations from both teachers and administrators and had ultimately internalized them. I recall one student telling me he had to have a grade higher than a C. When I responded that he should read the *Harbrace Handbook* from cover to cover and do as many of the exercises as possible, he stared at me in evident disbelief. I encouraged him to be gentle with himself and to expect to retain only perhaps sixty to eighty percent of his study but that with time and continual effort he would achieve a more sophisticated level of literacy.

Having started as a TA in the early 1980s when most students in writing classes received the C they deserved, I found it difficult to hand out largely all B's, while the pressure for all A's sent me looking for another way to make a living so as not to participate in the fraud of "higher" education. Misguided white guilt only complicates matters for serious, capable minority students and makes it all the more unlikely they'll be called upon to strive to develop their abilities to the highest degree possible. Steele perceptively touches on how university administrators are exacerbating this decline.

On another note, Steele states "to be human is to be responsible" and profoundly probes the intricacies of human motivation, responsibility, and the ways in which affirmative action and the thinking of politically correct race elites erode individual agency:

> Race should *never* play a role in social reform for many reasons, not least of which is that it is *always* used to help people avoid full agency for their fate. It always transforms the responsibility that free minorities should carry into a commodity that others will use for their own moral power. Race absolutely corrupts those who use it for redemption and absolutely weakens those who use it for advancement (112).

To all of which I say, "amen." I hope, indeed struggle to hope, that men like Shelby Steele, Ward Connerly, Thomas Sowell, and others will find the resources to continue to set a new course from the lamentable situation that plagues race relations today, especially in the university, though the struggle against patronizing white guilt for true individual responsibility and achievement exists in all walks of life. It seems to me that it is a struggle that must be fought primarily by intelligent blacks and minorities who have had enough of the insult of preferential treatment to stand up and fight for the unquestionable respect and honor they so rightly deserve and merit.

The Quest for Cosmic Justice
2000

Thomas Sowell may be one of the most despised black men in America—despised by extremist liberals, black and white, because Sowell has devoted his abilities to exposing their destructive ideologies of social redemption as counter productive to the best interests of all Americans. Widely known for his provocative, nationally syndicated newspaper articles and other books, he focuses, in *The Quest for Cosmic Justice*, on the misguided thinking behind the modern impulse to reform the very nature of the human condition from individual responsibility, competition, and performance to the tragic consequences of affirmative action and politicized egalitarian equality. Sowell locates the source of much of the problem in the academy, law schools, and government where "new elites" are quietly repealing the American Revolution. The "morally self-anointed," as he calls excessively liberal reformers and radicals,

> have for centuries argued as if no honest disagreement were possible, as if those who opposed them were not merely in error but in sin…. Given this exalted vision of their role by the anointed visionaries, those who disagree with them must be correspondingly degraded or demonized.

Marx, Lenin, Hitler, and Mao all followed this procedure, as have utopians of similar or less horrible results. That comparable dynamics rule the day, especially in the humanities in many American universities, will not surprise those who have any real experience of those departments. Sowell evokes the American political system and tradition in the hope of preventing its further erosion.

One of the many perceptive and striking points Sowell makes in the book involves "The High Cost of Envy." Pointing out its dangers broadly to poor people, he writes,

> The very terms of the discussion encourage them to attribute their less fortunate position to social barriers, if not political plots, and so to neglect the kinds of efforts and skills which are capable of lifting them to higher economic and social levels.

The acquisition of such "skills, education, discipline, foresight," needed to improve their lot, becomes less likely, as the "ideology of envy" blames others for exploitation and racism, undermining their own will to act, while rendering "more successful members suspect as traitors." Sowell observes this same "bogus explanation" can keep entire societies in poverty, making me think of my recent experience as an accredited participant at the United Nations Millennium Forum, May 22-26, 2000, where I witnessed Kofi Annan's wise proposal for a Global Compact with business swept aside and essentially replaced with the "sophisticated modern versions of the envy vision spread by the Third World intelligentsia, often seconded by the intelligentsia in more fortunate countries."

Summing up in a passage that has very wide application, Sowell states,

> Cosmic justice attempts to create equal results or equal prospects, with little or no regard for whether the individuals or groups involved are in equal circumstances or have equal capabilities or equal personal drives. To do this, it cannot operate under general rules, the essence of law, but must create categories of people entitled to various outcomes, regardless of their own inputs ... assuming with little or no evidence that only malign intentions or systemic bias could explain unequal results. 'Affirmative action' is

perhaps the classic example of this approach but it is only one example."

While his insight into the subtleties of modern ideologies is remarkable, as is his own high and demanding sense of justice, alas, I seriously found myself wondering at times if Sowell's *Quest for Cosmic Justice* is not a voice in the wilderness, as always, one come much too late. But I take heart in knowing such people as he, Shelby Steele, and Ward Connerly have the courage to speak out on race and other matters and in the end hope that events will unfold for the good in ways I can not imagine and that now seem so often unlikely. In this context, I recommend reading Robert Conquest's *Reflections on a Ravaged Century*, a parallel meditation on the dilemmas of modernity.

Black Rednecks and White Liberals
2005

The approval by voters of the Michigan Civil Rights Initiative corroborates Thomas Sowell's observation in his Preface to his book, referring to "a growing willingness to consider views that differ from the racial orthodoxy that has prevailed largely unchallenged from the 1960s onward in intellectual circles and in the popular media." The education, government, business, and media elites of Michigan all banded together to hammer into the population the same old tiresome racial orthodoxy, to no avail. The people had had over forty years of it, experienced it in lived life, and would have no more of it. By an overwhelming fifty-eight percent, they voted to change direction, try something different from the orthodoxy of the liberal elites. Thomas Sowell's book *Black Rednecks and White Liberals* suggests further lines for reconsideration and change.

In this context, I believe the most interesting essays in the book are "The Real History of Slavery" and "Black Education: Achievements, Myths and Tragedies." Rejecting the Kunte Kinte view of slavery found in Alex Haley's *Roots*, Sowell emphasizes that slavery was a worldwide phenomenon practiced by virtually all peoples and nations, not at all exclusively by white Western nations. Sowell perceives why the contemporary discussion of slavery is usually so distorted:

> Why would anyone wish to arbitrarily understate an evil that plagued mankind for thousands of years, unless it was not this evil itself that was the real concern, but rather the present-day uses of that historic evil? Clearly, the ability to score ideological points against American society or Western civilization, or to induce guilt and thereby extract benefits from the white population today, are greatly enhanced by making enslavement appear to be a peculiarly American, or a peculiarly white, crime (111).

All of this feeds directly into the radical politics of affirmative action racial preferences. It skews our understanding of the real historical evils of slavery and substitutes emotional Hollywood distortions for the complexity of human experience.

Narrowing the history of slavery from the long record reaching back over three thousands years, in Europe, Africa, China, India, every region of the world, it was nevertheless only the Western world that developed moral compunctions against slavery and launched a "bitter worldwide struggle, which lasted more than a century, to destroy the elaborate systems and institutions for the ownership and sale of human beings" (114). Of particular interest is Sowell's discussion of slavery under Islamic societies, in North Africa and elsewhere, which enslaved far more people than were ever brought to the Western hemisphere. Cervantes in *Don Quixote* has an incredible account of his five-year enslavement by Muslims after the battle of Lepanto in 1571. Sowell's discussion throws interesting light on the conditions to which European and African slaves found themselves subjected. Many millions of Europeans and Africans were enslaved over the centuries in Islamic countries, facts that ought to be studied much more after 9/11.

Similarly, Sowell emphasizes it was black tribal leaders who practiced slavery "before, during, and after the white man arrived" (120). Connecting the real history of slavery with its distorted uses by those who today want to fight for racial spoils, Sowell writes,

Yet what was peculiar about the West was not that it participated in the worldwide evil of slavery, but that it later abolished that evil, not only in Western societies but also in other societies subject to Western control or influence. This was possible only because the anti-slavery movement coincided with an era in which Western power and hegemony were at their zenith, so that it was essentially European imperialism which ended slavery.

This idea might seem shocking, not because it does not fit the facts, but because it does not fit the prevailing vision of our time (134-135).

Visions hang on beyond their time, beyond their usefulness, such has been the case with racial preferences, which are predicated on a distorted sense of actual historical slavery. By addressing the real history of slavery, Sowell restores the proper perspective needed to come to terms with the complexity of American slavery and the perspective needed to find new ways to work together today. He observes at one point "Africans did not treat Europeans any better than Europeans treated Africans. Neither can be exempted from moral condemnation applied to the other" (139). If Michigan is seeking a new understanding of equality, one place to begin might be to realize, as Sowell says elsewhere, the prevailing vision of slavery of the "morally self-anointed" is wrong. To find a new future, we must recognize our understanding of the past is flawed, reconsider its complexity, understand no one is blameless, and move forward together.

In "Black Education: Achievements, Myths and Tragedies," Sowell reconsiders the prevailing vision of the actual history of black education and demonstrates that it too is much different from the skewed account so many politically motivated radicals and liberals use to justify failed educational programs and policies:

The quest for esoteric methods of trying to educate black children proceeds as if such children had never been successfully educated before, when in fact there are concrete examples, both from history and from our own times, of schools that have been successful in educating black children, including those from low-income families. Yet the prevailing educational dogma is that you simply cannot expect children who are not middle class to do well on standardized tests, for all sorts of sociological and psychological reasons (203).

Sowell further states that this dogma is false for both black and other minority children and discusses a number of outstanding schools reaching from after the Civil War to the present, such as the M Street School, later to become known as Dunbar High School in Washington, DC.

After a long survey of these and other schools, Sowell writes,

> What the record of successful minority schools shows, both in history and among contemporary schools, is that educational achievement is not foredoomed by economic or social circumstances beyond the school grounds, as the education establishment constantly strives to prove. Poverty, broken homes, and unruly environments are not to be ignored, downplayed or apologized for. But neither are the failings of others proof that the education establishment is doing its job right. Perfect students with perfect parents in a perfect society cannot learn things that they are not being taught—and that includes an increasing number of basic things in our public schools (217).

While the howls of protest to this passage might be the usual ones from the education establishment, I would argue his stress on working with students where they are and expecting "work and discipline" (221) from them is a no-nonsense approach that ought to be tried more often than not, instead of the latest pitying, enabling, undermining educational theory that asks little or nothing of kids and gets little or nothing in return. Higher expectations of their families, whether single parent or not, ought to play a part, though Sowell dismisses the idea that without parental involvement there is no hope for the child, insisting that the individual student can take charge of his or her life and achieve despite the family situation.

Excoriating the victimhood approach to education, Sowell laments that "the history of successful black schools has attracted virtually no interest from either historians or educators. That history does not advance any contemporary political agenda, though it might help advance the education of a whole generation of black students" (225). Far from blaming all educational problems of black students on racism, the usual liberal scapegoat, Sowell has no patience with such facile excuses and lays the blame squarely on the students themselves: "By and large, black students do not work as hard as white students, much less Asian students" (228). He goes on to blame a culture of non-achievement, comparing it to red-neck and lower-class whites and Asians who suffer from "the same counterproductive attitudes toward education" which are "just as self-defeating." Failure is not restricted to any particular pigmentation or race, nor are the real reasons for such failure always unique to any particular race.

In a fine section of this chapter on education, Sowell highlights the views of Booker T. Washington and W. E. B. Du Bois, documenting that their attitudes on educational expectations and other matters were much closer than the common politicized opinion today would have it. The necessary resources and exemplary individuals run rife throughout black history and experience. I would add what is also needed is for more people to hear and respect such scholars as Thomas Sowell, learn from them, and work together to chart a new path together into the future.

In his conclusion Sowell essentially challenges educational leaders and students "to work harder and abandon the counterproductive notion that seeking educational excellence is 'acting white'" (244). The problems are known. The black community is in crisis and needs to take action:

Despite the heartening achievements of some black schools, which have repeatedly demonstrated what is possible even with children from low-income backgrounds, the general picture of the education of black students is bleak. Much of what is said—and not said—about the education of black students reflects the political context, rather than the educational facts. Whites walk on eggshells for fear of being called racists, while many blacks are preoccupied with protecting the image of black students, rather than protecting their future by telling the blunt truth. It is understandable that some people are concerned about image, about what in private life might be expressed as: "What will the neighbors think?" But, when your children are dying, you don't worry about what the neighbors think (245).

Though bleak, attitudes are changing, will continue to change, will, as Ward Connerly has remarked, take time to change, creating a new climate of expectations and performance, on all sides. The passage of the Michigan Civil Rights Initiative registers such change. Neighbors of goodwill do exist, are distressed, worried, and concerned, willing to help, where they can, if allowed. It needs to be said much more often that 14% of black voters approved the proposal. They are people who want much of what Sowell discusses in terms of education for their children and community. These two essays ought to be read by anyone serious about assessing where we are after the passage of the Michigan Civil Rights Initiative, and where, together, we are all going from here.

For Betty—Oh God,
What Have We Done?
June 16, 2000

One brings to a book everything one is and has been through. Let me discuss David Horowitz's *Hating Whitey: And Other Progressive Causes* by seemingly digressing a little on my own experience. I grew up in the white suburbs of Detroit during the `60s and `70s and have vivid memories of the Detroit riot and my uncle and aunt's bakery being almost burnt to the ground, while their neighbors and friends were increasingly driven out by violence and the erosion of social order. In the end, they too accepted the inevitability of flight for their lives. More than forty years of programs and promises of "renaissance" have only produced a dysfunctional city that often can neither educate its young nor reliably provide the most basic services such as snow removal and, for a couple of days now, electricity.

At the University of Michigan I studied with Robert Hayden, a former Consultant in Poetry at the Library of Congress, who thought of himself as a human being, first and foremost, though he begrudgingly accepted Afro-American, despite his preference at times for Negro, coming from an older time. The child of an interracial marriage, Hayden loathed the divisiveness of racial politics and lacerated radical blacks on more than one occasion. Ultimately, his vision of human oneness melded with that of Martin Luther King and similar figures, challenging us all to a deeply demanding spiritual ethic, a universal standard holding all accountable, before which all must struggle and strive.

David Horowitz devastatingly chronicles the result of the lack of such a standard on race relations during the last forty years; the result in the university; the result in the media; the result in the legal system; the result in politics; the result in the hearts and minds and souls of our entire nation.

As someone who has edited the poems and prose of a human being usually identified as black, I have had the experience several times of being invited for job interviews at colleges only to be met with disbelief and gaping mouths when I, a "whitey," walked in through the department door. I am one who has lived through almost everything about which Horowitz writes regarding academia, including losing a tenure track job as the result of a relentless and byzantine conspiracy of "colleagues" who wanted a black in the position, one widely perceived by those fit to judge as nowhere near my intellectual equal and who eventually had to be removed from my post for incompetence.

Horowitz's major shortcoming, typical of the modern secular mind, liberal or conservative, is that his critique, unlike Dostoevsky who understood the nature of modernity, does not go deep enough into the spiritual collapse that underlies the dynamics of race, as they underlay the collapse into communism. This failure is also evident in his *Destructive Generation*, which is, nevertheless, another of his brave and brilliant books. Perhaps someday Horowitz will plumb further into the depths of radical causes. (Actually, he has informed me, his autobiography *Radical Son* does touch on his ambivalence towards Judaism and religious belief, leaving him ultimately "stubbornly agnostic.")

Being a white man, Horowitz demonstrates a rare streak of moral strength and courage by his daring to speak his conscience against black racism and the misguided designs of race elites. Fortunately, he is not alone.

John McWhorter's *Winning the Race: Beyond the Crisis in Black America* has a strong sociological approach to the issues of black America, surveying the history of the development of the inner cities and the welfare system, leading to the dependence that later found expression in affirmative action and racial preferences. My background being more literary in nature, I do not have the grounding for assessing McWhorter's sociological arguments and data and will focus on his discussion of racial preference and its dynamics, of which I have personal experience, on the ground shall we say, and, hence, extensive knowledge and interest.

Referring to radical race elites and leaders, McWhorter states,

> What people like this are seeking is, sadly, not what they claim to be seeking. They seek one thing: indignation for its own sake. And that means that the alienation that they are expressing is disconnected from current reality (5).

Highlighting the psychological drive of the protest impulse, McWhorter continues,

> This is therapeutic alienation: alienation unconnected to, or vastly disproportionate to, real-life stimulus, but maintained because it reinforces one's sense of psychological legitimacy, via defining oneself against an oppressor characterized as eternally depraved (6).

He refers often throughout the book to the implicit theater entailed in such attitudes and the misguided strategy of relying on such theater for advancement and self-definition, instead of "rolling their sleeves up and working out concrete plans for change" (7). Putting aside the emphasis of more traditional black leaders, such as Booker T. Washington and W. E. B. Du Bois, on personal responsibility and initiative, increasingly after the 1960s civil rights generation, "the main culprit was whitey and his 'systemic racism'" (13). I cannot help feeling it's an old story, but, one that cannot be told too often, still today, given the continuing mutual recrimination and the evasion of the obvious.

The more interesting chapters to me deal directly with affirmative action, racial preference, and the serious damage done by race elites allowing for years the continuation of the "acting white" mentality to spread and pollute the springs of self-reliance, independence, and education for black youth, in their innermost consciousness:

> To understand that we are dealing with therapeutic alienation rather than racism brings us to implications for grappling with the black-white achievement gap in the present and future…. To set the bar lower for black students out of a sense that the achievement gap is due to socioeconomics is mistaken. Because the factor is not socioeconomic but cultural and self-perpetuating, the lowered bar only deprives black students and parents of any reason to learn how to hit the highest note. Much of the time, there is not even any way for black people to know what it would actually be to perform at that level—because they never have to (263).

A devastating critique of a devastating system, one that all people, white and black, have participated in creating and maintaining, much to the detriment of ourselves and our young people. McWhorter's honesty about racial matters and race preferences is truly admirable. How else can we all come to understand what the situation truly is and then decide what to do about it? Alas, one can almost count on one hand the scholars intelligent and honest enough to state simply the truth about many "black students on campus":

> So few of them have grades or test scores high enough to qualify under the regular evaluation procedure. In response to claims from the occasional whistleblower that standards are being lowered for black students, administrators are trained to insist that this is not true. Yet, simple and readily available data show that each year, there is but a sliver of black students with the grades and test scores considered sine qua non for serious consideration if students were white or Asian (264).

Laying the blame squarely on "teen culture" and the failure of black and white parents and leaders to have sufficiently high expectations for all students, McWhorter faces what virtually no one else in America will. It's our fault. We've got the pernicious system we've created, along with all the social and personal destruction that goes with it. I like the way he puts it at one point: "a new sense of black identity in the sixties has led to a quiet cultural disconnect from the 'school thing'" (273). Instead of "self-defeating cultural patterns," McWhorter argues for the cultural patterns that produce success for all people. For decades, Caribbean and African immigrants, Asian boat people, and others who have entered urban schools have flown past the kids held back by the misguided ideas of the race elites: "As long as black students have to do only so well, they will do only so well" (295). Like Ward Connerly, John McWhorter clearly advocates expecting more of black kids, knowing only then can society and educators elicit from students their highest potential.

In the light of the Michigan Civil Rights Initiative (MCRI) and the misleading allegations surrounding gender that have been used to scare white females into voting against it, McWhorter asks a simple question that Michigan women ought to consider: "Whites listening to defenses based on 'diversity' should ask themselves a simple question: Would you allow this of your own children?" (308). Cutting to the quick and ending his book on the hopeful note that black kids are every bit as capable of competing and achieving as anybody else, McWhorter quite rightly states, lampooning radical race elites who benefit from the affirmative action gravy train, "The simple fact is that America is quietly getting past race despite the best efforts of the Soul Patrol to pretend otherwise" (377).

The work of John McWhorter ought to be even more widely known than it already is in Michigan and throughout the country. On November 8th, Michigan's concerned citizens should turn more to his understanding of what went wrong and what is required for success.

If the University of Michigan is truly interested in the equal opportunity and success of black students, I invite my alma mater to organize a conference, a summit of people who have two feet on the ground, as soon as possible after November 8th, with the following keynote speakers, hosted by U of M Professor Carl Cohen: Ward Connerly, Thomas Sowell, John McWhorter, Shelby Steele, Juan Williams, and Michigan State University Professors William B. Allen and Carol M. Allen.

Ending racial preferences in Michigan and throughout the Nation is essential for creating an atmosphere of high and equal expectations for all our children, capable of Winning the Race, in all senses of the phrase. Together we will find our way towards a new meaning of what it is to be an American, as did Ralph Ellison in *Invisible Man*, not white *or* black, but white *and* black, and all the shades of humanity beyond.

CPSIA information can be obtained
at www.ICGtesting.com
Printed in the USA
BVOW06*0243110817
491592BV00011B/75/P